An Interpretation of Goya's Caprichos

An Interpretation of Goya's Caprichos

Jeanne Smith Morgan

**80 line drawings
suggesting the essence of the Caprichos
with captions in English and
the original antique Spanish
of Francisco Goya**

Cover illustration from Capricho # 21

Line drawings and Introduction by Jeanne Morgan

Reference for line drawings and text: Third edition of Los Caprichos
in the collection of Dr. William Emboden

Foreword by William S. Emboden, Ph.d., F.L.S., Professor Emeritus,
California State University at Northridge

English translation by Julian Palley, Ph.d., Professor Emeritus,
Department of Spanish and Portuguese, University of California at Irvine.

Technical production by Robert Bissett, Bs.Arch.
Layout & preparation for publication by Loi Eberle, MA, CPC
Meadowcreek Press
248 Kootenai Trail, Naples, ID 83847

ISBN 9781468194715

CONTENTS

FOREWORD

California artist, Jeanne Morgan, has created a worthy homage to Goya's *Los Caprichos* in a new medium, that of line drawing.

Los Caprichos is Francisco Goya's enigmatic portfolio of 80 aquatints, combined with etching, commenting on the follies and evils of the eighteenth century corrupt and despotic society of wealthy Spanish aristocrats. Goya depicts the suffering of the impoverished, a despicable clergy and church, witchcraft, superstition and all the bizarre features of a social order emerging from conditions that included the Spanish Inquisition. *Los Caprichos* is the heart and center of all Goya's works of creative genius.

As a work of art, *Los Caprichos* is rich in lights and darks achieved by a combination of etched line and aquatint which presents a ground of ink in fissures made by dusting areas of a copper plate with crushed resin. A sharp implement, pressed into this ground, makes the linear drawing and etched shading to create dense blacks.

However magnificent the result, there is still room for extracting from these images their very essence in the form of line drawings. It is this, the vitality of line, that we remember in the graphic works of artists such as Picasso and Matisse. But why? Because line drawing, when it is pure and certain, is also poetry. It is that which makes a work "sing."

Morgan has shown us the passion of one who can do just that. Long involved in studies of Goya, she took up a dip pen and India ink and, each day for 80 days, "translated" one capricho into the poetry of sparkling line drawing, thus producing the 80 drawings of *An Interpretation of Goya's Caprichos*

Every line of Morgan's homage is a telling interpretation from which entire images are reborn in today's world. There is an irony in the contemporary applicability of these swift, revealing lines parodying ignorance, vice, the wealthy, those in power and both despotism and populism.

In Morgan's opinion, the arts have a right to be free of political influence, which can reduce them to propaganda. At the same time they have the right to address political and social issues that affect human welfare. The challenge is to remain an artist and to do so with aesthetic impact. Goya teaches us this. It is a lesson much ignored in today's art climate, where trivia often triumphs. Goya would have had a trenchant comment on that.

Like the originals in 1799, *An Interpretation of Goya's Caprichos* bites at the ignorance and vices of our time. It includes bilingual, often stinging comments. Those in antique Spanish are by Goya himself, from the Prado manuscript. The bold, gutsy, English translation is by Julian Palley, Ph.d., professor emeritus, Department of Spanish and Portuguese, University of California at Irvine.

In the drawings of Jeanne Morgan we are invited to study a true and certain hand, one that has captured all the nuances of her subject.

An Interpretation of Goya's Caprichos is a gateway to Goya, himself; an open door to the magnificent mysteries of his work.

WILLIAM S. EMBODEN, Ph.d., F.L.S.
Professor Emeritus
California State University at Northridge

Introduction

A country boy, Francisco José Goya y Lucientes was born to a poor family in the village of Fuendetodos near Saragossa, on March 31, 1746. His enterprising father was a peasant who became an artisan gilder of picture frames. His mother believed she had royal connections. When he was 14, Goya was apprenticed to a Saragossa painter, where he showed talent, but he was not a child prodigy. Later he studied painting in Madrid and Italy.

His vibrant country background and bohemian lifestyle showed its vitality in his youth for then he was involved in romances, brawls, hasty departures to escape the police, a trip to Italy with a gang of matadors, helping a nun escape her convent. The full truth of these years cannot be found, but his escapades indicate Goya's rich involvement with life, which appears 30 years later in his prints.

When he was about 25, Goya finally settled down in Madrid, where he married the sister of an established painter, who helped him find his way into aristocratic circles. Thus he was appointed a tapestry designer and began a long career working for the Royal Manufactory of Tapestries for palace walls. Curiously, his themes were not the garden parties of the nobility like other designers, but slices of realistic life, the life around him. He designed witty scenes of donkey drivers, washerwomen, musicians, peasants and artisans in the marketplaces and boulevards of Madrid His paintings were wholly realistic in both form and content.

Ten years later he had advanced his status. He was a popular portrait painter, with a diverse group of clients: the rich and famous, scholars, royalty, picadors and courtiers.

His career leaped forward once again in 1789 when he was appointed a court painter to King Charles IV. In that year the Parisians imprisoned their king and stormed the Bastille. The power of the Enlightenment and the French Revolution were in full force.

But backward Spain offered an extreme contrast in its social structure which was 100 years behind the rest of Europe where the Enlightenment was turning men's minds away from a dark supernatural world and toward the light of reason. In Spain the Inquisition was still capturing women as witches and burning them at the stake in public squares. The people were illiterate and bound in superstition. The Inquisition and an absolute monarch ruled over a country still mired in medieval darkness.

Social criticism was not yet Goya's concern. Perhaps he was beginning to rebel inwardly but outwardly he played his role as a famous painter. His manner was the same as everyone in his privileged circle. Nothing he produced suggested an active social awareness.

He was living a luxurious life in high style with his own carriage and servants. Traveling among the aristocracy in 1790, he fell in love with a central personage of the nobility, the Duchess of Alba. Her response did not endure, although Goya painted several superb portraits of her, including the most famous, "The Naked Maja."

Perhaps stung by the Duchess of Alba's rejection, Goya left Madrid in 1792 and went to visit his hometown of Saragossa. There he fell desperately ill, so severely that his friends believed that he could not recover; his illness lasted for two years. When he recovered he was totally deaf and his eyesight was damaged. This deaf, half blind artist could not write a letter, to say nothing of his inability to paint.

During his recovery from his deadly illness he read about the French Revolution and its ideals. He emerged from his sickness a changed man, bitter, solitary, somber and haunted by disturbing dreams.

Thus it was during the last year of his recovery, in 1794, that Goya began his most famous work, the suite of 80 etchings entitled *Los Caprichos*: the whimsies, the fancies, inventions. Goya claimed and used the artist's creative imagination and the psychological power of suggesting the truth that underlies fantasy. Everything in the *Caprichos* is suggested, hidden, implied, whispered, but hinted at. When human forms cannot carry the message, Goya invents monsters with their strong ability to suggest or hint at evil.

With the *Caprichos*, Goya became a messenger for his people and for humanity. He attacked the decaying order of the church, the establishment and the Spanish Inquisition. The *Caprichos* show him at the critical beginning stage of his growth as a revolutionary artist. His hellions, witches and phantoms are not the ravings of a sick mind but carefully chosen symbols capable of conveying social criticism in a disguised form, rendered in etching and aquatint.

To work with such perverse content and subject matter was revolutionary and it made him a target of the Inquisition. Not only the content but the form of his new art was revolutionary because previous artists had used the aquatint method only to reproduce pale French watercolors. Goya combined aquatints with etchings to produce a wide range of tones from white to deepest velvety blacks.

The etching process involves blocking out a copper plate using varnish or resin and then, with a sharp tool, drawing into the surface to reach the metal. An acid bath reaches through the drawn areas and cuts the metal which will then catch the ink. The resin remains and is removed by solvents. Each plate is then inked, wiped and printed on a hand press.

Goya's aquatints were produced on the same plate, by an etching process capable of producing several areas of tones by varying the etching time. The plate is coated with a field of powdered, melted pine resin, then areas are blocked off to make darker and lighter tones. The plate is then heated in order to melt the resinous powder. The degree of heat must be controlled to produce differing tones of dark and light. This, too, is removed by solvents, making the plate suitable for the printing press after inking and wiping.

Goya's technical methods are as enigmatic as his images of demons and devils. The plates are aquatints, yes, but they are also etchings. They might properly be called etched aquatints because an enormous amount of drawing is seen in every print except Plates 32 and 39 which have no drawing, no black lines. They are pure aquatints. Half blind, Goya could still manage these close-up exacting techniques.

From an artist's view the creator of *Los Caprichos* was a passionate inventor whose profound concern to communicate with his audience gave him the strength to pursue the long, technically complex processes that produced his extraordinary etched aquatints.

Goya uses chiaroscuro (light and shadow) powerfully to express the emotional content of the images. Fine gradations of black to white provide backgrounds of shadowy clouds or fantastic creature-shapes and phantoms.

Philip Hofer advises, in the Introduction to the Dover edition of *Los Disparates*, "It would seem best to look at these prints without trying to discover any specific meaning – to loosen one's aesthetic emotion and to allow one's unfettered imagination to revel in or be stirred by the train of thoughts and emotions the prints evoke." The same may be said of the *Caprichos* plates.

Los Caprichos was first published on February 6, 1799. The first print in the series is a self portrait, at the age of 50, a profile in which the artist looks askance, his lower lip protruding, as if he is experiencing an unpleasant smell. It is a comment on the disquiet he feels about the subjects that follow.

Goya considered *Los Caprichos* to be a "universal language," a means of communicating his new insights to his fellow men. Literacy was not required.

In the first half of the volume things happen as they might in real life; a mother frightens her child with superstition, a child is abused, a masked man and woman lie to each other, a superstitious woman touches a corpse, a bride is sacrificed to a depraved man to gain family wealth, a tart is accosted by a beggar who turns out to be her mother.

Goya deals with wickedness and evil in his everyday world. Nobody knows anybody but vices are equal in men and women. Women are seduced, degraded, sacrificed. Men and women fleece each other. Persecution by the Inquisition exists while women are also harmed by surgeons and the police. A privileged elite reigns over all and is portrayed as jackasses.

Nearly a quarter of the prints deal with the vicious conditions of women's lives. Goya knew about the most personal of women's concerns and presented them in subtle ways that escape an insensitive viewer, but he knew his audience for such matters. He speaks, in ink and accompanying texts, against lewdness, drunkenness, greed and gluttony; he examines and reveals perversities and dehumanized relations of the sexes: prostitutes pluck their victims but are caught in the courts themselves. In Plate 24 a prostitute is being led to her death by the Inquisition. But burning her alive is a crime greater than her own crime. The satisfied authorities smile, the crowd is wild with glee and excitement. "There was no other remedy," so they killed her. Which is the worse crime? Such questions are posed by the images.

With Plate 37 a series of jackass images begins. Like many other Caprichos, here Goya is satirizing a specific person; the ass studies with an older teacher, he is entertained and catered to as he grows older, he is driven by a passion to get ahead in society (thus his deep study of genealogy). This is a reference to Godoy, the Queen's favorite, who is next seen as a specious doctor unable to cure. Then the ass is painted and flattered. Finally the elite asses are carried on the backs of the common people and this little story series ends. The moral is clear: The common people are enduring and supporting such jackasses.

The second half of the *Caprichos* opens with Plate 43, the famous print, "The sleep of reason brings forth monsters." Our translator, following the theme of Aldous Huxley's translation in the Crown edition of *Los Caprichos,* renders the text as: "The sleep of reason brings forth monsters. Fantasy, without reason, may make monsters, but reason itself, without imagination, may create even worse demons. Imagination, deserted by reason brings forth impossible monsters. United with reason she is the mother of the arts and the source of their wonders."

With intense imaginative power, Goya offers satirical and ironic dreams and visions of witches and hellions with an expressive realism that sees creatures as realistic, actual beings: demons learning their witchcraft, vampires, vicious cats, bats, monstrous birds, plucked chickens, quarreling dogs, simpering apes and monkeys, an arrogant parrot, a basket full of dead babies, bulls, a skull, a snake, a snarling tiger, a huge owl wearing the glasses of the Law, men and women with bodies of birds and chickens, women and phantoms who fly through the air; supernatural beings with enormous power. The Duchess of Alba flies aloft, supported by witches. Here Goya presents a daring criticism of the Catholic Inquisition.

With these phantoms Goya shows the true face of his world, ripping off the masks of a degenerate society. He was living among people whose religion required that they believe in a hell-spawn of evil spirits and supernatural beings. A heresy, such as doubting the monsters of hell, was severely punished by the Inquisition.

Daring the wrath of the Inquisition, Goya presents monks as representatives of the church, servants of the Inquisition. He shows their rites, their triumphs and their treasured informers who appear in the backgrounds often in shadow. There are several portrait/caricatures that seem to be references to his contemporaries, as well as infernal monsters and demons as forms of the arts of witchcraft. He excoriates forced marriage, child abuse and people who believe in supernatural power.

Goya was not "that poor mad Spaniard," but a volatile artist with a political program. His images were cast so far beyond normal realism that they sing with fresh vigor and provocation even today. His strikingly terse comments bring out the meaning and power of the images.

When he was 53 years old in 1799, his folio of *Los Caprichos*, which he had worked on for five years, went on sale at a perfume and liquor shop whose owner was probably a sympathetic friend. The sale lasted 48 hours, during which time 27 copies of an edition of 270 books were sold. (Multiplication by his 80 plates will show how much hard work it took to print such a large edition by hand.)

But this small, powerful book caught the attention of malicious friends of the Inquisition. Goya, personally, removed all copies after only two days on sale. Clearly there was good reason for the enigmatic captions. The book was secreted for a time until the suspicions against the artist were quieted. Four years later the King, who had befriended Goya, took possession of the remaining edition and all the copper plates. Perhaps the King was so unsophisticated that he failed to detect the double meanings in Goya's satirical work. Thus *Los Caprichos* was saved for the future.

Original prints made by Goya in that first edition and subsequent printings may be seen today in museums and private collections. The Prado Museum in Madrid has a suite of limited preliminary drawings executed in sanguine chalk. Thus we see evidence that the *Caprichos* were carefully thought out.

During the 30 years of his life after the *Caprichos*, Goya produced other thematic suites: *Los Disparates* or *Los Proverbios* is similar to the *Caprichos* in that the images are fantastic, but they are more specific. Each image relates to a certain proverb.

Los Desastres de la Guerra contains shocking images of the brutality of war which Goya witnessed as Napoleonic troops invaded and occupied Madrid and slaughtered the citizenry during the Peninsular War of 1808-1814. *La Tauromaquia* is a suite of etched aquatints in which people kill bulls and bulls kill people. All these works are darker, more somber than the *Caprichos*. *Los Desastres*, in particular, offers chilling scenes of the killing of civilians.

During his life after the *Caprichos*, Goya produced a group of huge paintings on the walls inside his country house, using the style of fantastic images which were his invention. Here phantasmagorical witches and ghouls appear in color, dissolving into dense black surroundings. Known as the "Black Paintings", they were cut down from the walls a half century after Goya's death and taken to exhibit in Paris, in Madrid, then to the Prado, where they remain today.

Even more psychically disturbing than the *Caprichos*, these 14 big paintings include a huge black goat-sorcerer who looms over a crowd of frightened people, lecturing them. A witch-crone stirs a bowl of black food while a skeleton looks on, begging. Hovering creatures appear: a mournful dog, and the shocking picture of Saturn devouring one of his children. Indeed, this disturbing figure might be seen as rabid madness until one remembers a contemporary reality that updates Goya's fantasy: our own government sends its youth to be devoured – in endless wars.

It seems bewildering that Goya's subjective reality can be so horrendous, yet we see beauty in *Los Caprichos*. This is surely a testament to the mastery of his work. Among the monsters are images so enigmatic that one must admire the wondrous imagery while the social message is sometimes too embedded for contemporary understanding.

Is there no current artist (has there been one since Goya?) who can create penetrating moral meaning out of the horrors we live with? Picasso tried, with the famous Guernica painting, but the cartoon form overcomes the humanist content and we genuflect in puzzlement because we have been told it is the greatest antiwar painting. But does it move us to terror and pity?

Perhaps Theordor Adorno was right when he said that there can be no art after Auschwitz. What could contemporary culture offer in equality with Goya? Perhaps there is no such artist because Goya saw that the controversial is of interest and importance and he had the courage to depict it. Much art, in our time, with important exceptions, is mired in trivia, not controversy; it has scant emotional impact.

Whatever judgment is made of *Los Caprichos*, no one can accuse anything in Goya's work of being trivial. He acknowledged only three teachers: nature, Rembrandt and Velasquez. He stands on the threshold of the modern age with his revolutionary and creative leap in which he defined himself as speaking against convention. He is a divide between the Inquisition, the new age of Enlightenment and the love of reason.

In our society it would require attention to many social ills to create something analogous to Goya's *Caprichos*. Necessary targets would be topics such as people who hunger for power, the churches molesting their children, corporations buying politicians, capitalism free to seek profits at the expense of the planet and banks robbing the poor and taking their homes. Attention would have to be paid to the grotesquely super rich who hold the main fortune of the nation and to the working class, abandoned as businesses move overseas to gain cheap child labor. The very rich sequester their gold in bullion as the nation sinks into a debt of trillions. It is now that we need Goya.

Goya's revolutionary character is seen in his desire to use art for a new purpose: not a collaboration with royalty and the establishment, but for the enlightenment of his audience in matters of social justice and truth.

In 1824 Goya left his country house, its walls covered with malevolent and savage paintings, and moved into self-exile in Bordeaux, France where he lived until his death in 1828 at age 82. It is interesting to note that his friend, Antonio de Brugada, a liberal Spanish painter, fled the country to escape political persecution and went to Bordeaux a year before Goya, in 1823. Perhaps Goya was not entirely alone in his exile. He died there on April 16, 1828.

What was he: an artist, a caricaturist, a cartoonist, a social critic, a satirist, an inventor? A man as complex in his nature as the symbolic, mysterious images of his work, he alone was brave enough to portray Spain's horrors, knowing that he might be killed for revealing so many monstrosities.

He was, above all else, a brave genius who cared so much about the people's welfare that he risked his safety to tell the truth about the evil world he lived in.

We intend this book of interpretations as an invitation to explore all of Goya's works in their original, magnificent form. Prowl the libraries and seek out Francisco Goya.

Jeanne Morgan, MFA
Santa Barbara, California

vii

LIST OF CAPTIONS

1. Francisco Goya, painter
   Francisco Goya y Lucientes, Pintor

2. They say yes and give themselves to the first who offers.
   El si pronuncian y la mano alargan al primero que llega.

3. The boogieman will get you!
   ¡Que viene el Coco!

4. The Mamma's boy.
   El de la Rollona.

5. What a pair!
   Tal para qual.

6. It's all a masquerade.
   Nadie se conoce.

7. He can't figure her out.
   Ni así la distingue.

8. They kidnapped her!
   ¡Que se la llevaron!

9. Tantalization.
   Tantalo.

10. Love and death.
    El amor y la muerte.

11. The gang's all here.
    Muchachos al avío.

LIST OF CAPTIONS

LIST OF CAPTIONS

24. There was no help for it.
    No hubo remedio.

25. Sure, he broke the pot.
    Si quebró el Cántaro.

26. They have plenty to sit on.
    Ya tienen asiento.

27. Which of them is the most overcome?
    ¿Quien mas rendido?

28. Shh!
    ¡Chiton!

29. He is certainly reading.
    Esto si que es leer.

30. Why keep hiding them?
    ¿Porque esconderlos?

31. She prays for her.
    Ruega por ella.

32. Because she was sensitive.
    Por que fue sensible.

33. To the Count Palatine.
    Al Conde Palatino.

34. Fast asleep!
    ¡Las rinde el sueño!

35. A close shave!
    ¡Le descañona!

LIST OF CAPTIONS

LIST OF CAPTIONS

LIST OF CAPTIONS

LIST OF CAPTIONS

72. You won't escape.
    *No te escapar*ás.

73. It's better to be lazy.
    Mejor es holgar.

74. Don't scream, stupid!
    ¡No grites, tonta!

75. Can't someone untie us?
    ¿No hay quien nos desate?

76. Watch out! Make way...look out! or else…!
    ¿Esta um...pues, como digo...eh?¡Cuidado! ¡Si nó!

77. One to another.
    Unos á otros.

78. Hurry, they're waking up!
    ¡Despacha, que dispiertan!

79. No one has seen us!
    ¡Nadie nos ha visto!

80. It's the hour! Time to be off.
    ¡Ya es hora!

THE DRAWINGS

1. Francisco Goya y Lucientes, painter

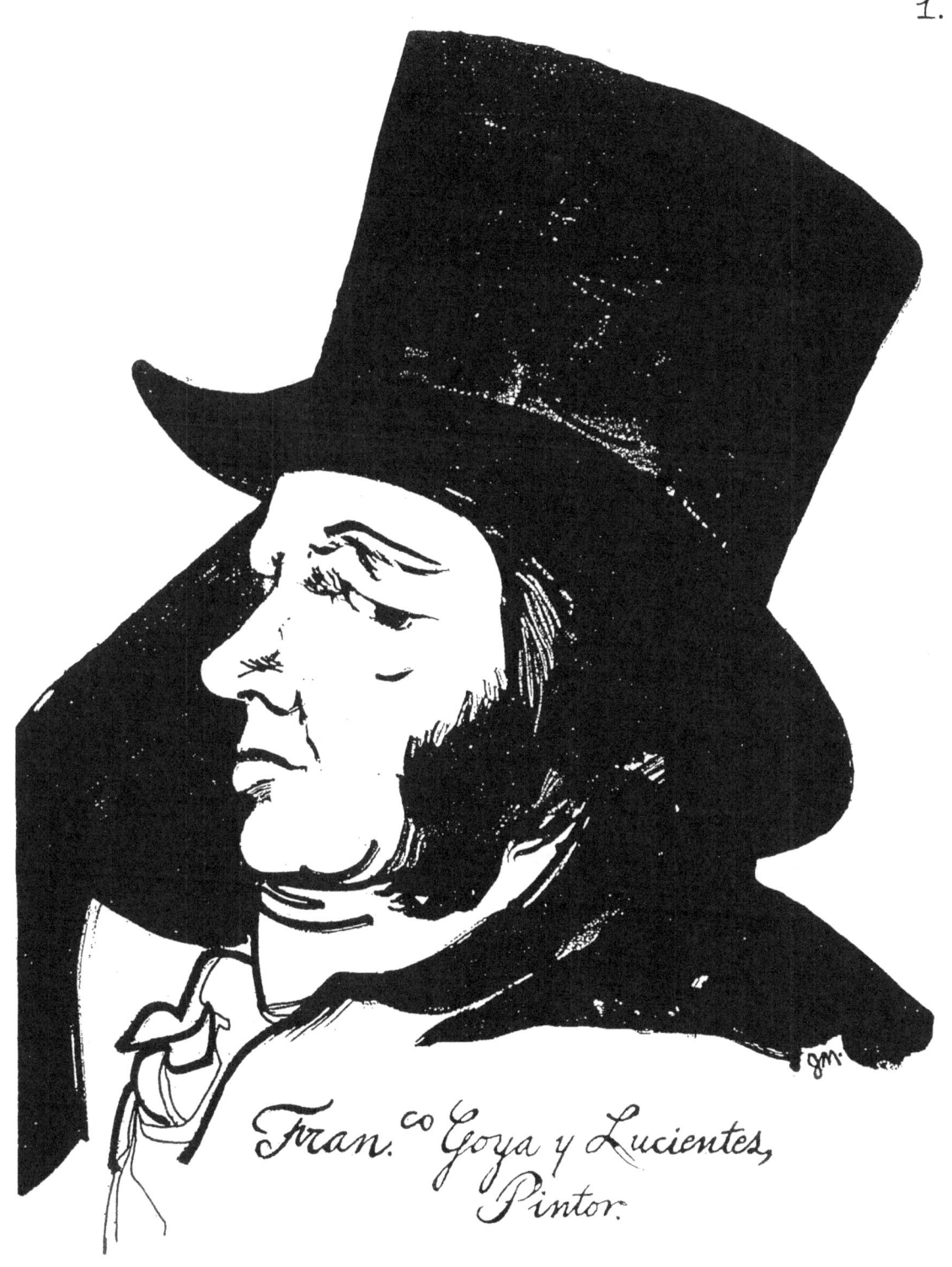

Fran.^{co} Goya y Lucientes,
Pintor.

2. They say yes and give themselves to the first who offers.
   Many women are ready to marry the first fellow who shows up, believing that marriage will give them a life of more freedom.

El si pronuncian y la mano alargan al primero que llega.
Facilidad con que muchas mujeres se prestan á celebrar matrimonio esperando vivir en él con más libertad.

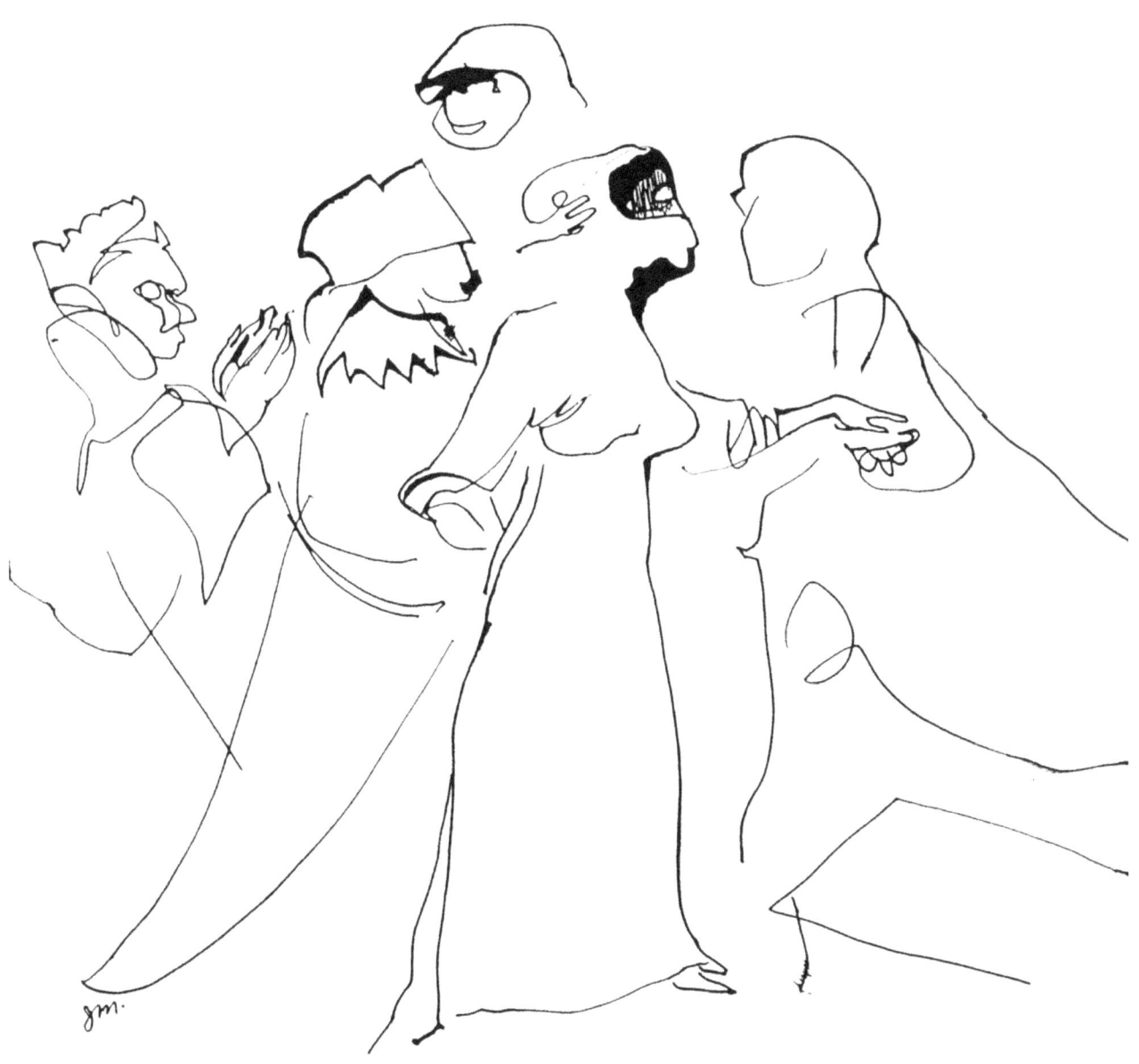

2

They say yes and give themselves to the first who offers.

3. The boogieman will get you!

What a miserable way to educate a child — to fear the boogieman
more than his own father and to make a youngster afraid of a superstition.

¡Que viene el Coco!

*Abuso funesto de la primera educación. Hacer que un niño tenga más
miedo al Coco que a su padre, y obligarle á temer lo que no existe.*

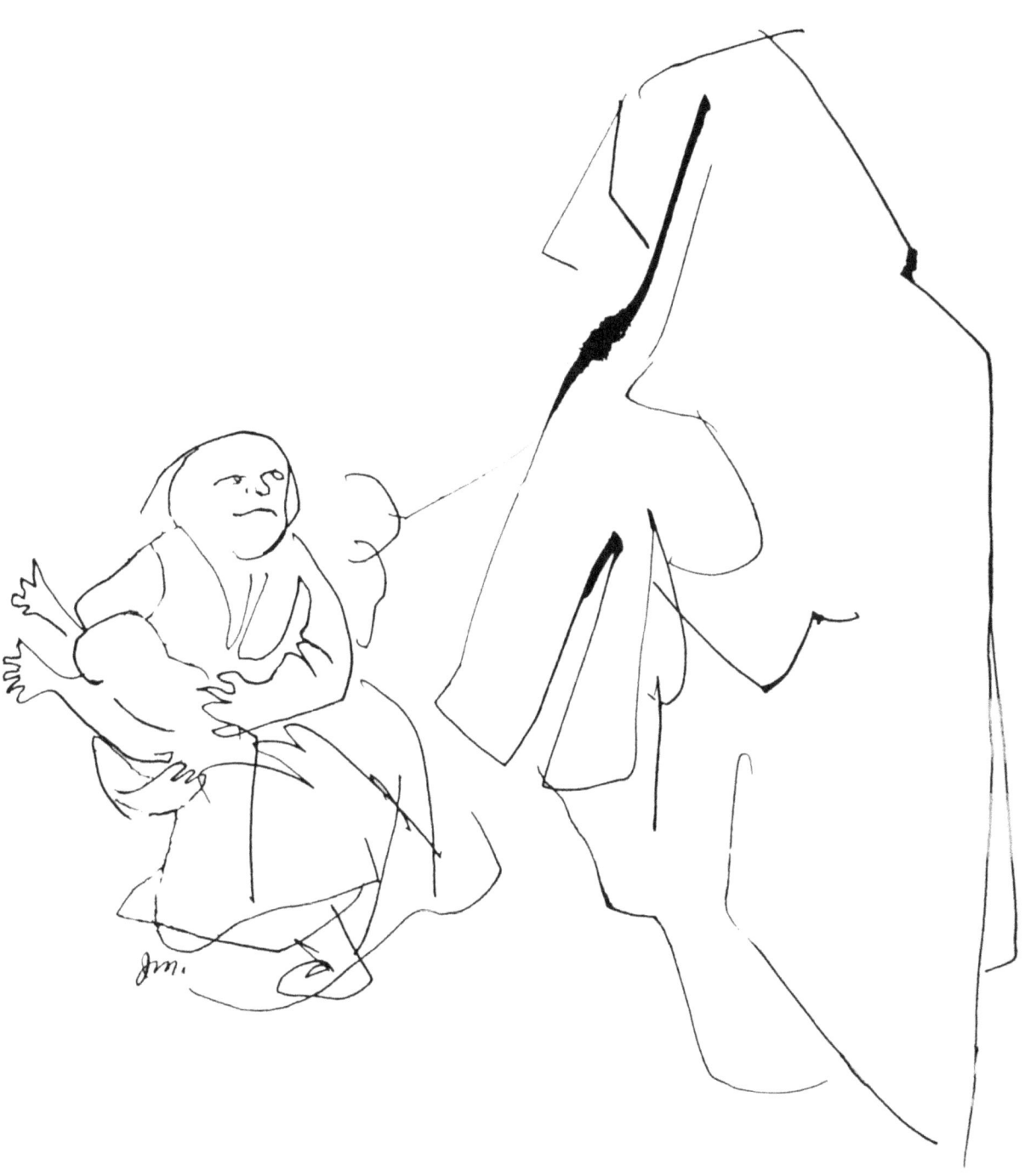

3

The boogieman will get you!

4. The Mamma's boy.

Neglect and indifference make children spoiled, obstinate, lazy, naughty, greedy and insufferable. They grow up but still act like a child. Thus the Mamma's boy.

El de la Rollona.

La negligencia, la tolerancia, y el mimo hacen á los niños antojadizos, obstinados, soberbios, golosos, perezosos, e insufribles; llegan á grandes y son niños todavia. Tal es el de la Rollona.

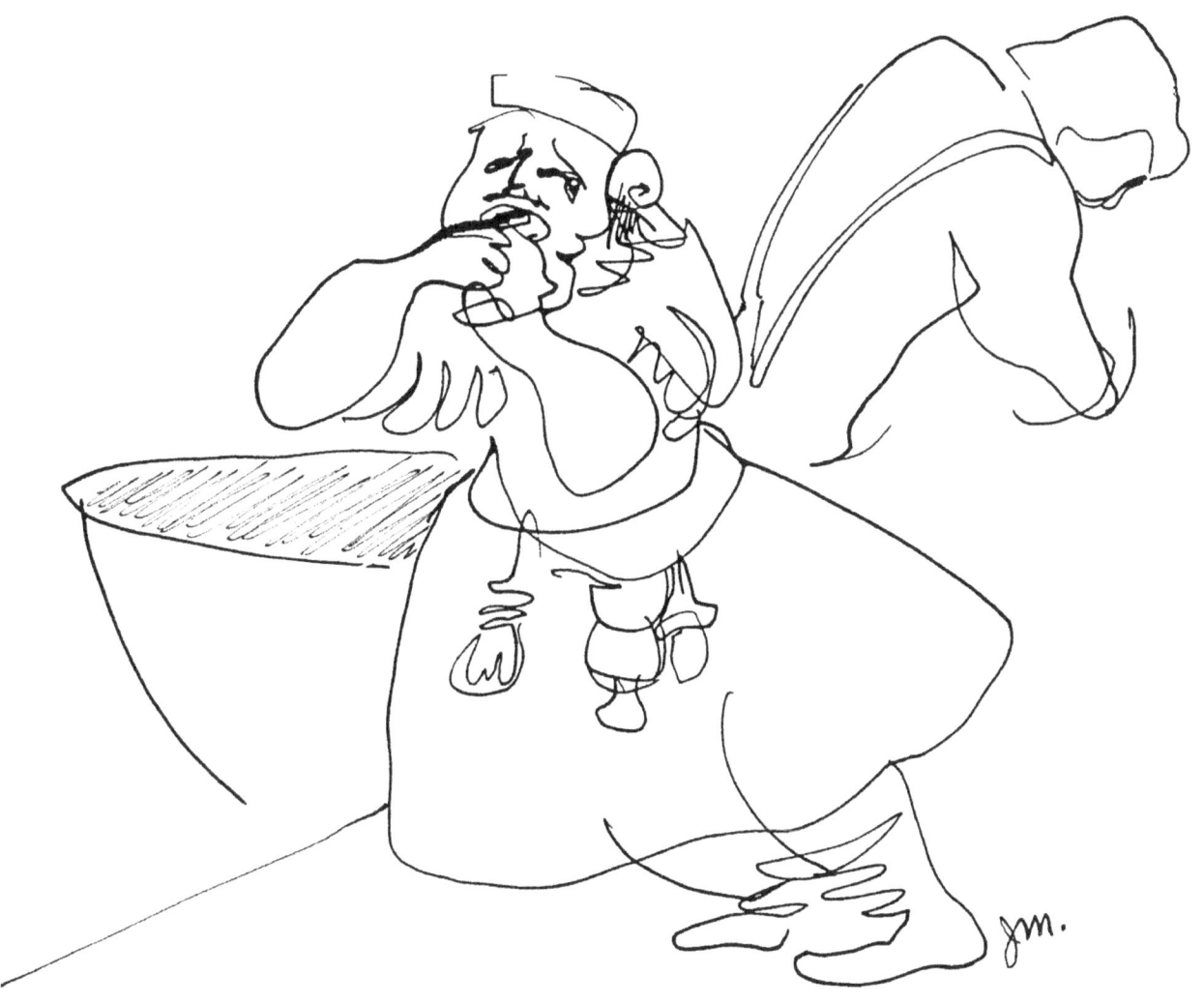

4

The Mamma's boy.

5. What a pair!

People argue about whether men are worse than women,
or just the opposite; but their vices come from the same bad upbringing. If
the men are depraved the women will be also. The girl
talking to the fellow in this print is as depraved as he is. As for the
old hags, one is as vile as the other.

¡Tal para qual!

*Muchas veces se ha disputado si los hombres son peores que las
mujeres o lo contrario. Los vicios de unos y otros vienen de la mala
educación; donde a quieran que los hombres sean perversos, las
mujeres lo serán también. Tan buena cabeza tiene la señorita que
representa en esta estampa como el pisaverde que le está dando
conversación, y en cuanto a las dos viejas tan infame es la una como
la otra.*

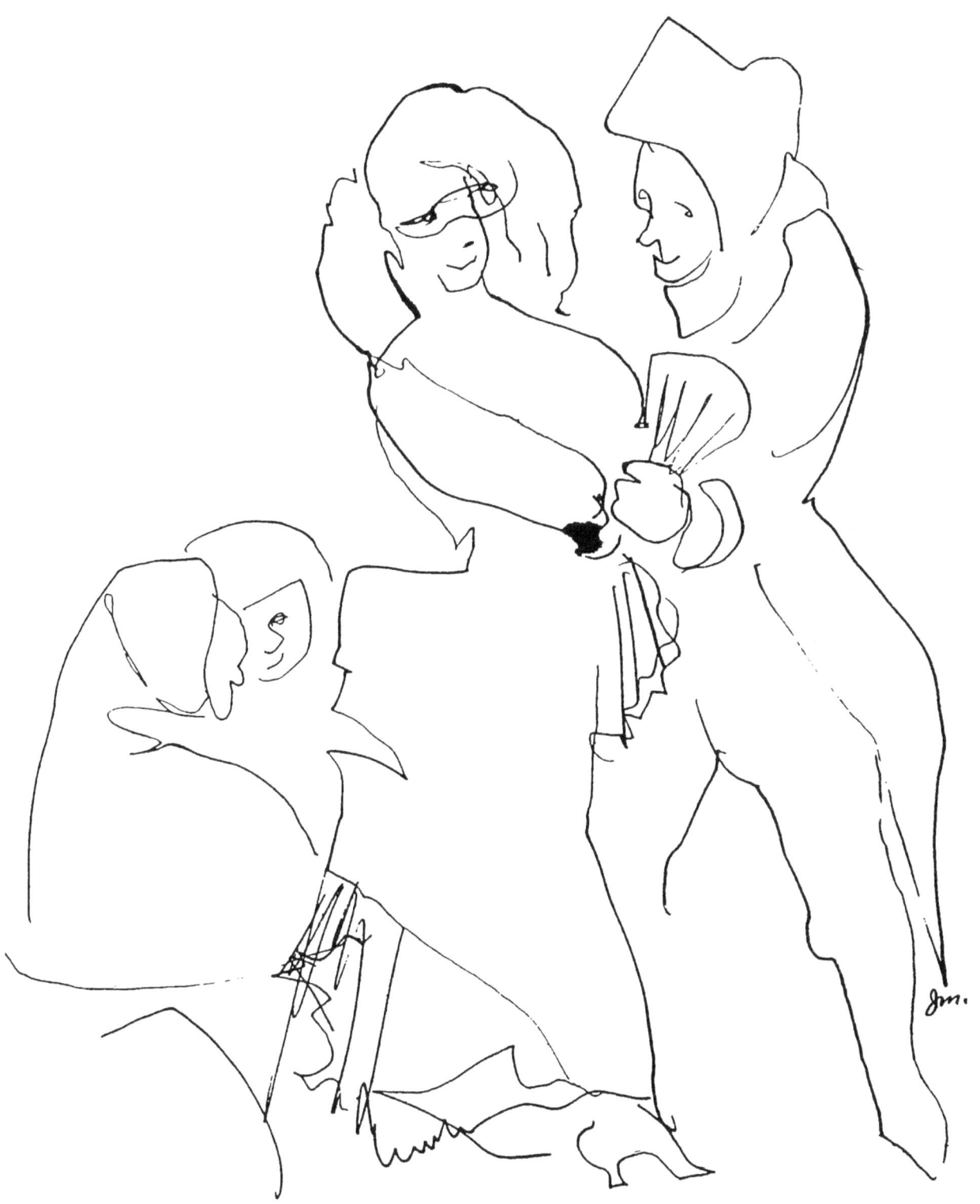

5

What a pair!

6. It's all a masquerade.

Everything is false, the clothes, the face, the voice. Every
one disguises himself but doesn't know his own true nature either.

Nadie se conoce.

El mundo es una máscara, el rostro, el trage y la voz, todo es fingido.
Todos quieren aparentar lo que no son, todos engañan y nadie se conoce.

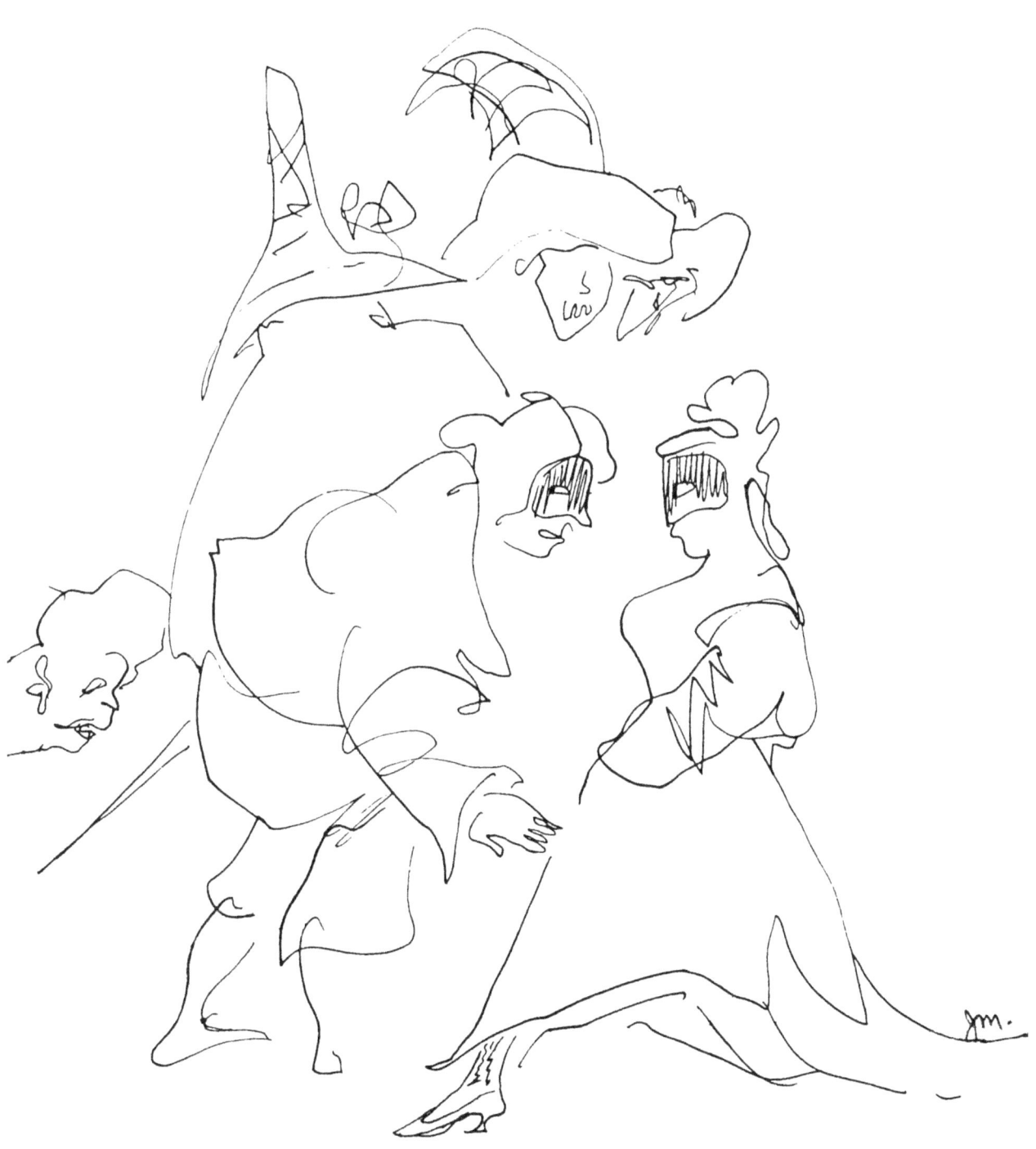

6

It's all a masquerade.

7. **He can't figure her out.**

A monocle is not enough to find out what she is. One needs worldy experience and good judgement; just what this poor fellow doesn't have.

Ni así la distingue.

Como ha de distinguirla? Para conocer lo
que ella es no basta el anteojo; se necesita juicio y prática de
mundo y esto es precisamente lo que le falta al pobre caballero.

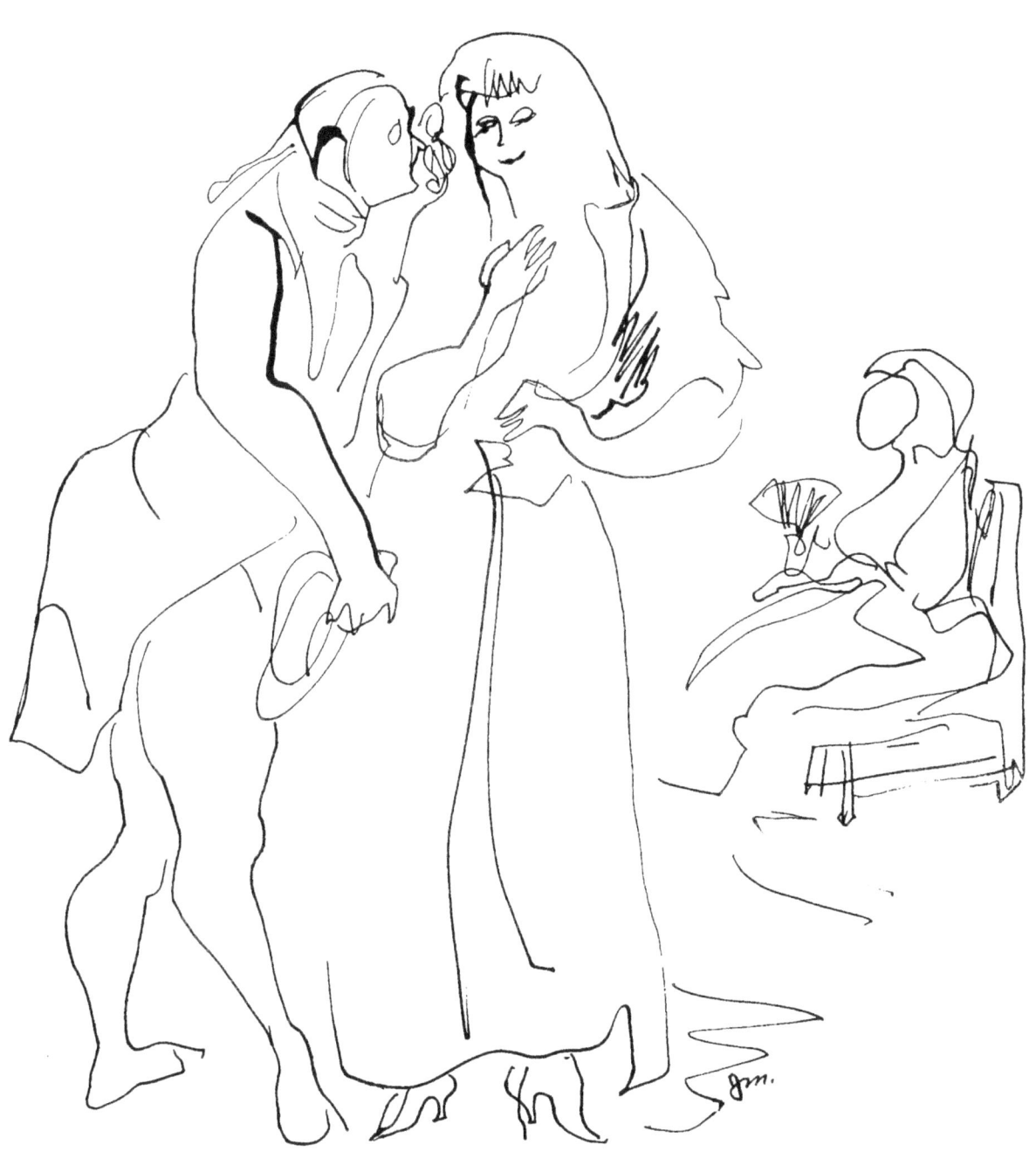

7

He can't figure her out.

8. They kidnapped her!

A woman needs to be cautious and take care of herself or she'll be carried off. When this has happened people are surprised that she has disappeared.

¡Que se la llevaron!

La mujer que no se sabe quardar es del primero que la pilla y quando ya no tiene remedio se admiran de que se la llevaron.

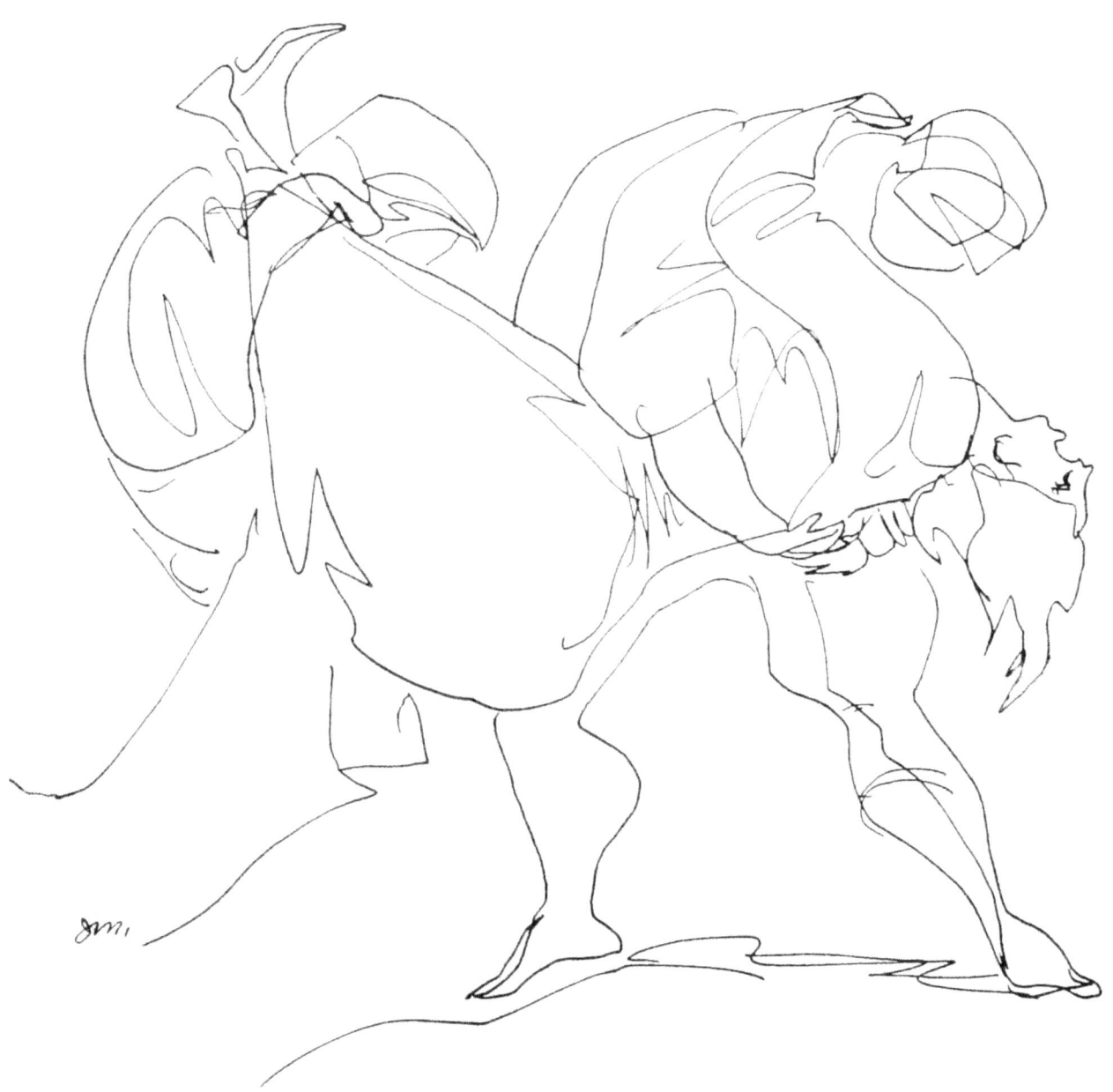

They kidnapped her!

9. Tantalization.

If he were a more passionate lover and less delicate she would revive.

Tantalo.

Si el fuese mas galán y menos fastidioso, ella revivirla.

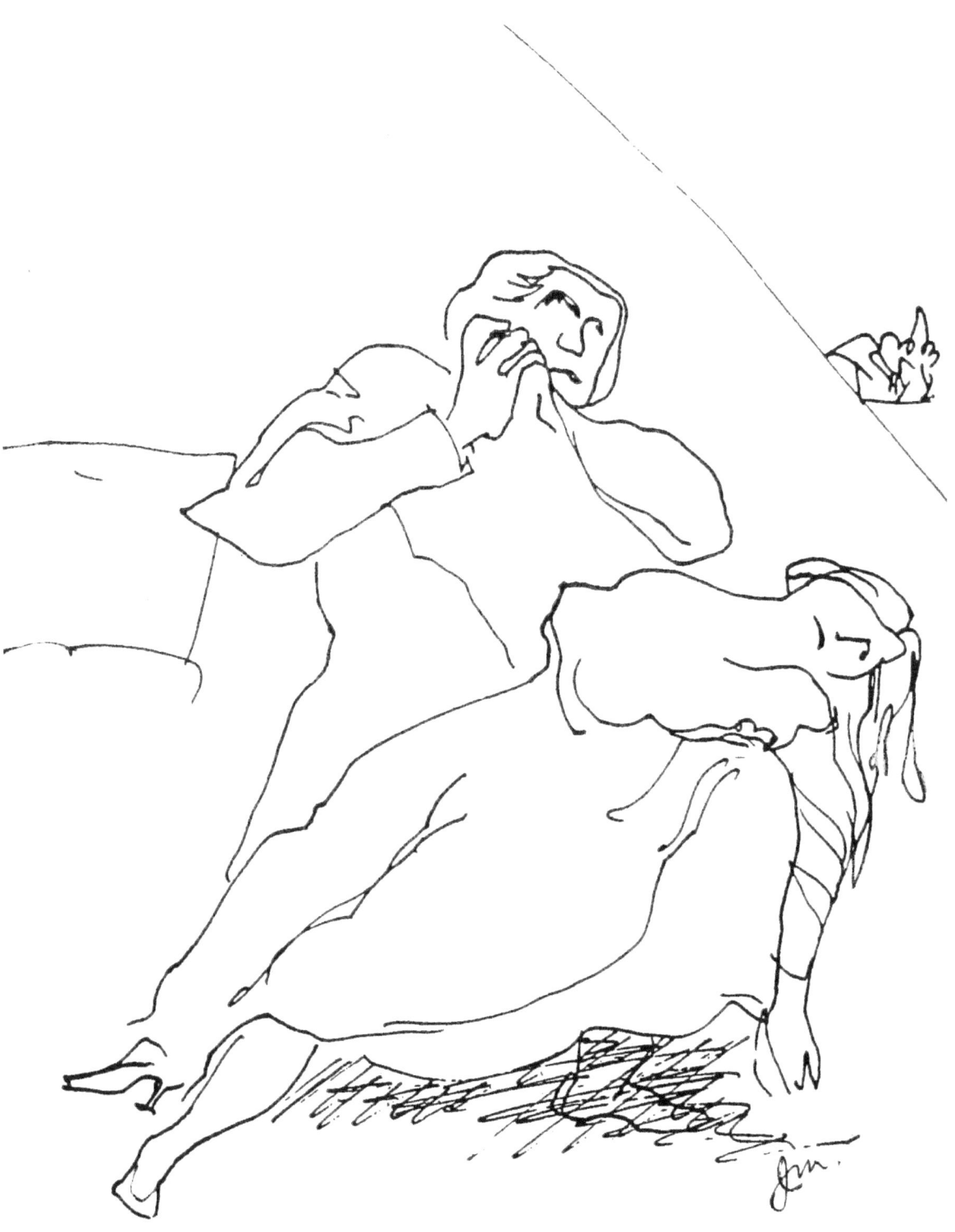

Tantalization.

10. Love and death.

See here a lover who has drawn swords with his rival and lost the game. Now he is in the arms of his beloved, but not for long. It is not smart to draw the sword too often.

El amor y la muerte.

Ve aqui un amante de Calderón que por no saberse reir de su competidor muere en brazos de su querida y la pierde por su termeridad. No conviene sacar la espada muy a menudo.

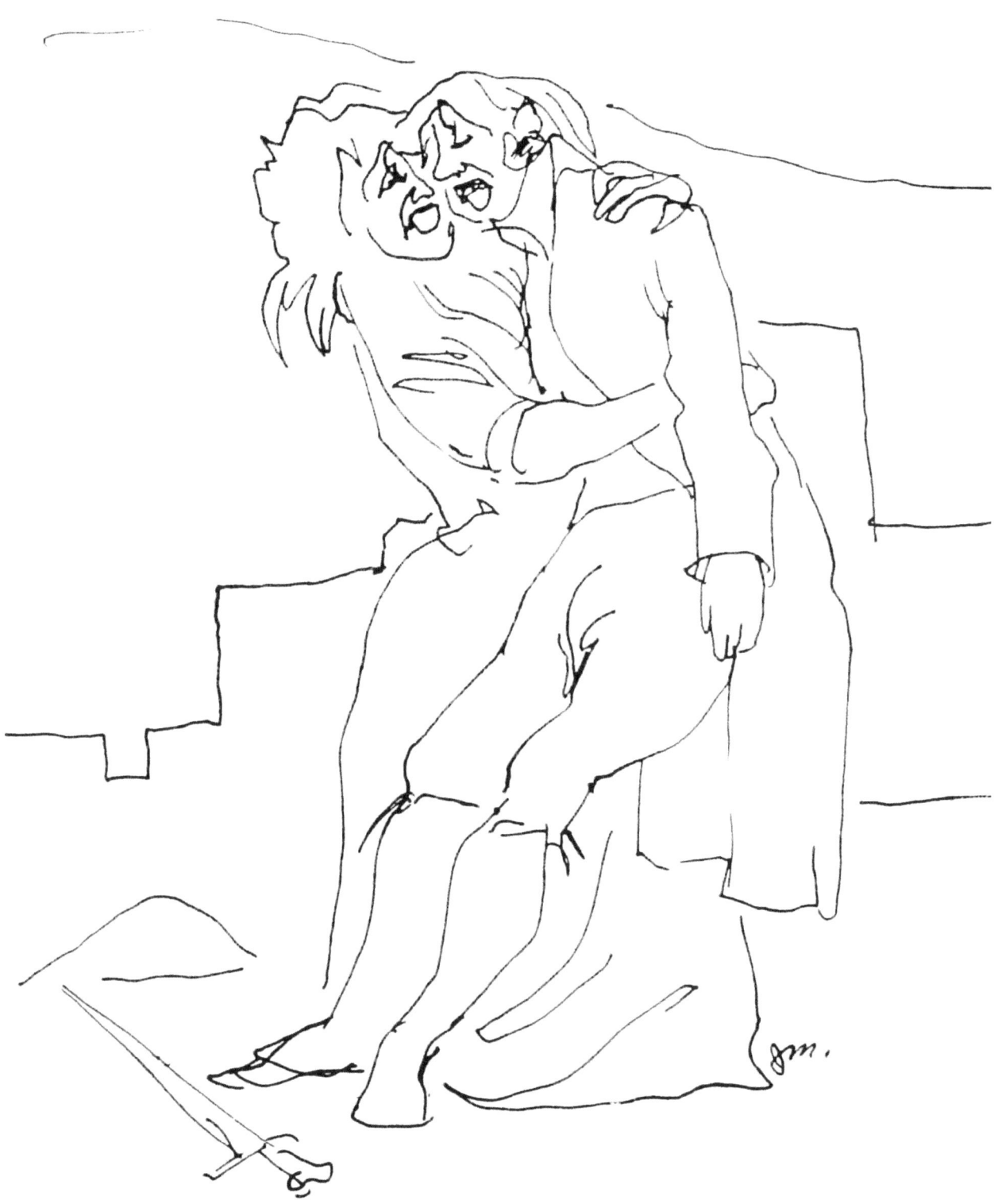

Love and death.

11. The gang's all here.

You can see what kind of scum they are by their clothes and faces.

¡Muchachos al avío!

Las caras y el trage están diciendo lo que ellos son.

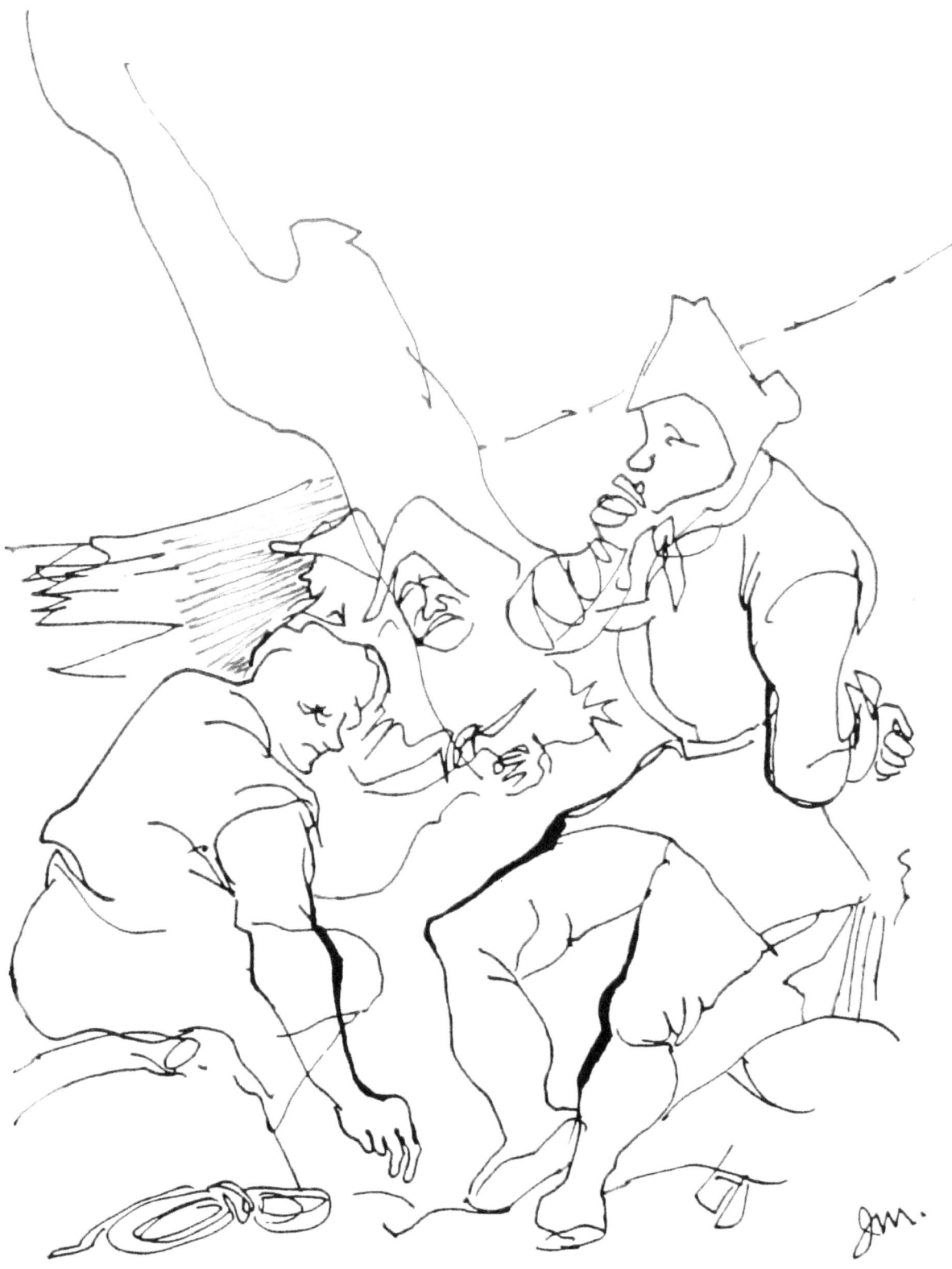

The gang's all here.

12. Collecting teeth.

Sorcery works best if you have some teeth from a hanged man. Too bad that ordinary people believe in such superstitious nonsense.

A caza de dientes.

Los dientes de ahorcado son eficacísimos para los echizos;
sin este ingrediente no se hace cosa de probecho. Lástima
es que el vulgo crea tales desatinos.

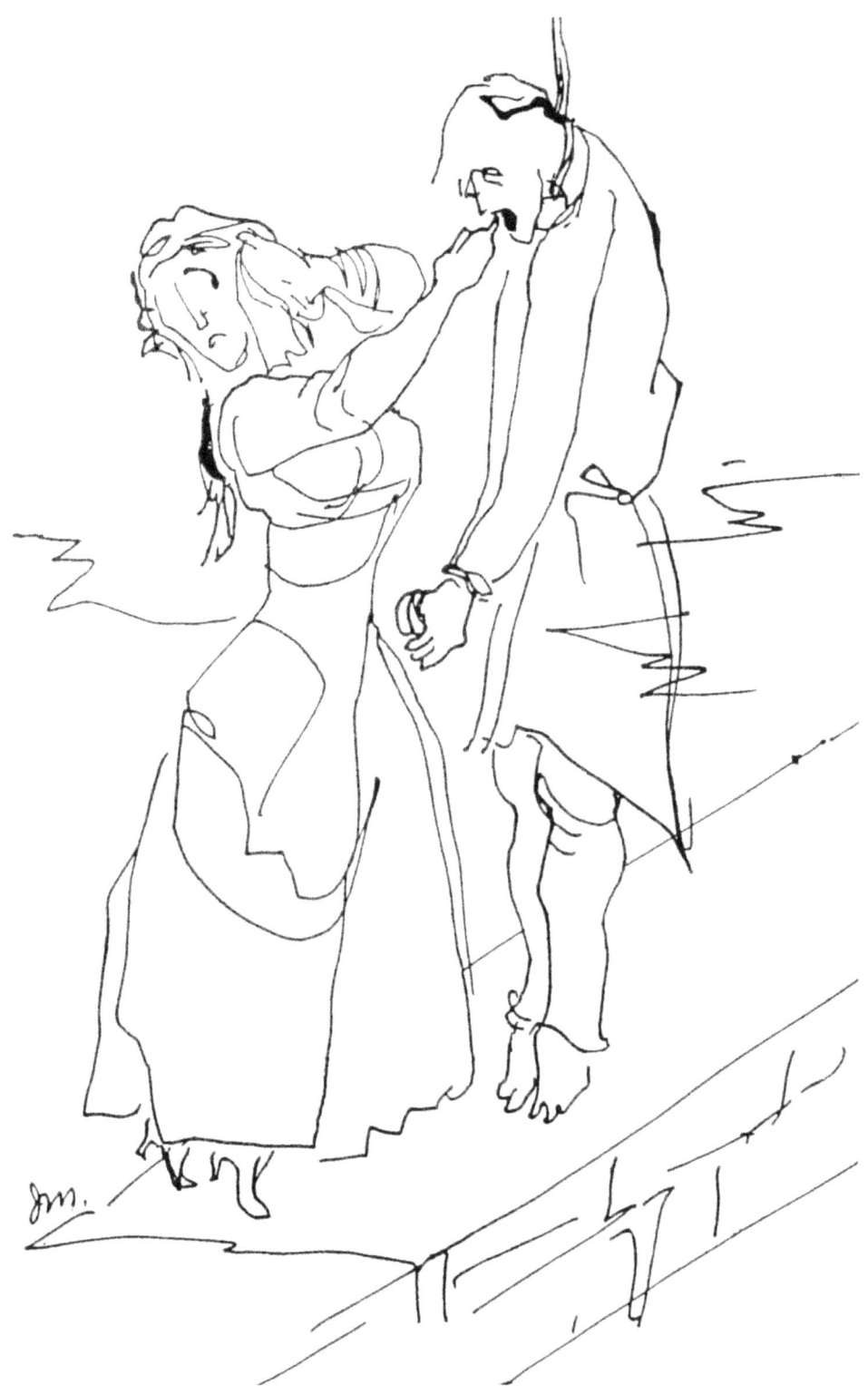

12

Collecting teeth.

13. Burning hot.

They swallow it burning hot because they are in such a hurry to swill it down. Restraint and balance are necessary even in pleasure.

Estan calientes.

Tal prisa tienen de engullir que se las tragan hirbiendo. Hasta en el uso de los placeres son necesarias la templanza y la moderación.

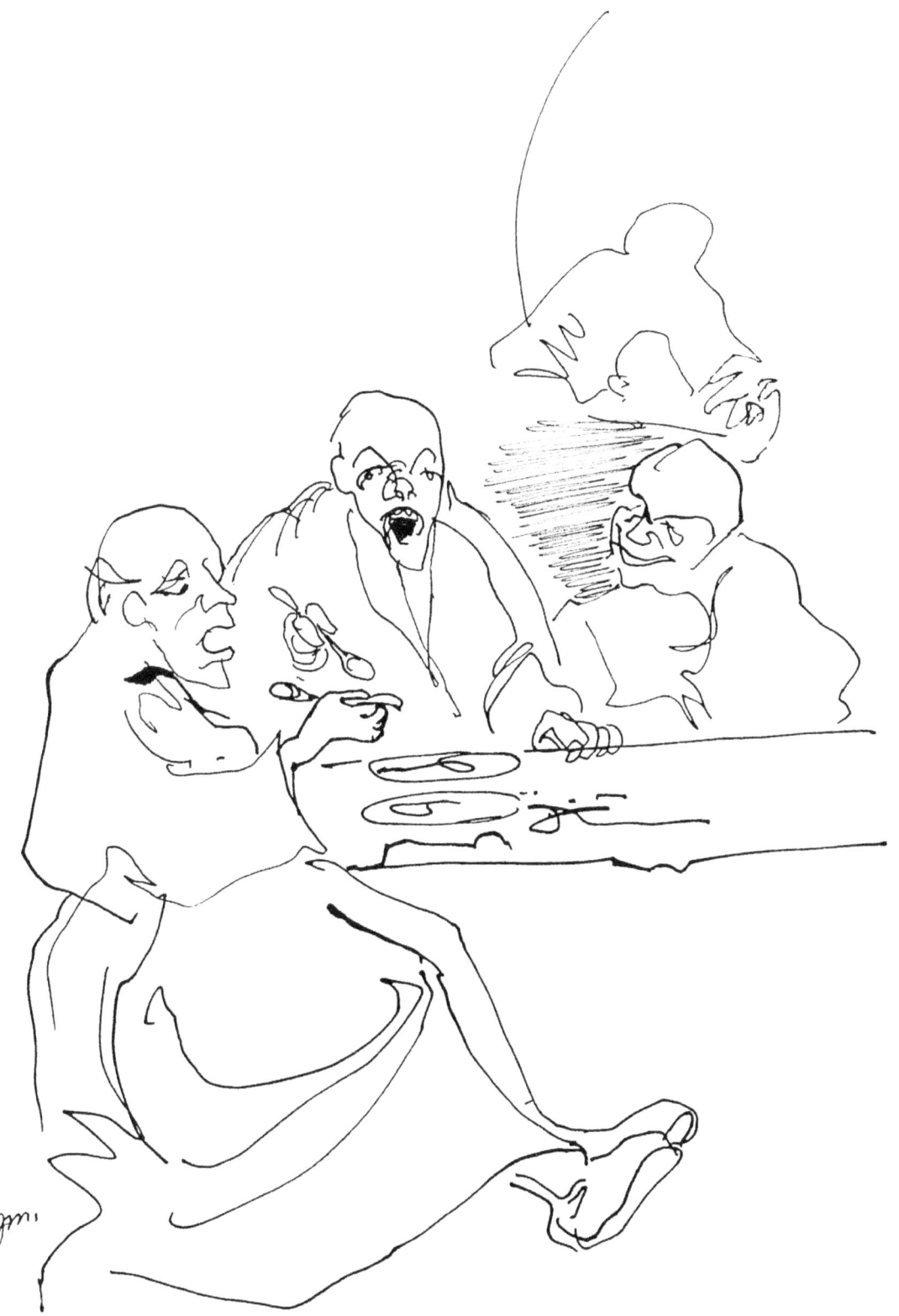

13

Burning hot.

14. What a sacrifice!

The family doesn't care that the groom is disgusting, since he is rich and
will support all of them at the cost of a young girl's happiness. So it goes!

Que sacrificio!

*Como ha de ser el novio no es de los más apeticibles, pero es rico y a costa
de la libertad de una niña infeliz se compra el socorro de una familia
hambrienta. Así va el mundo.*

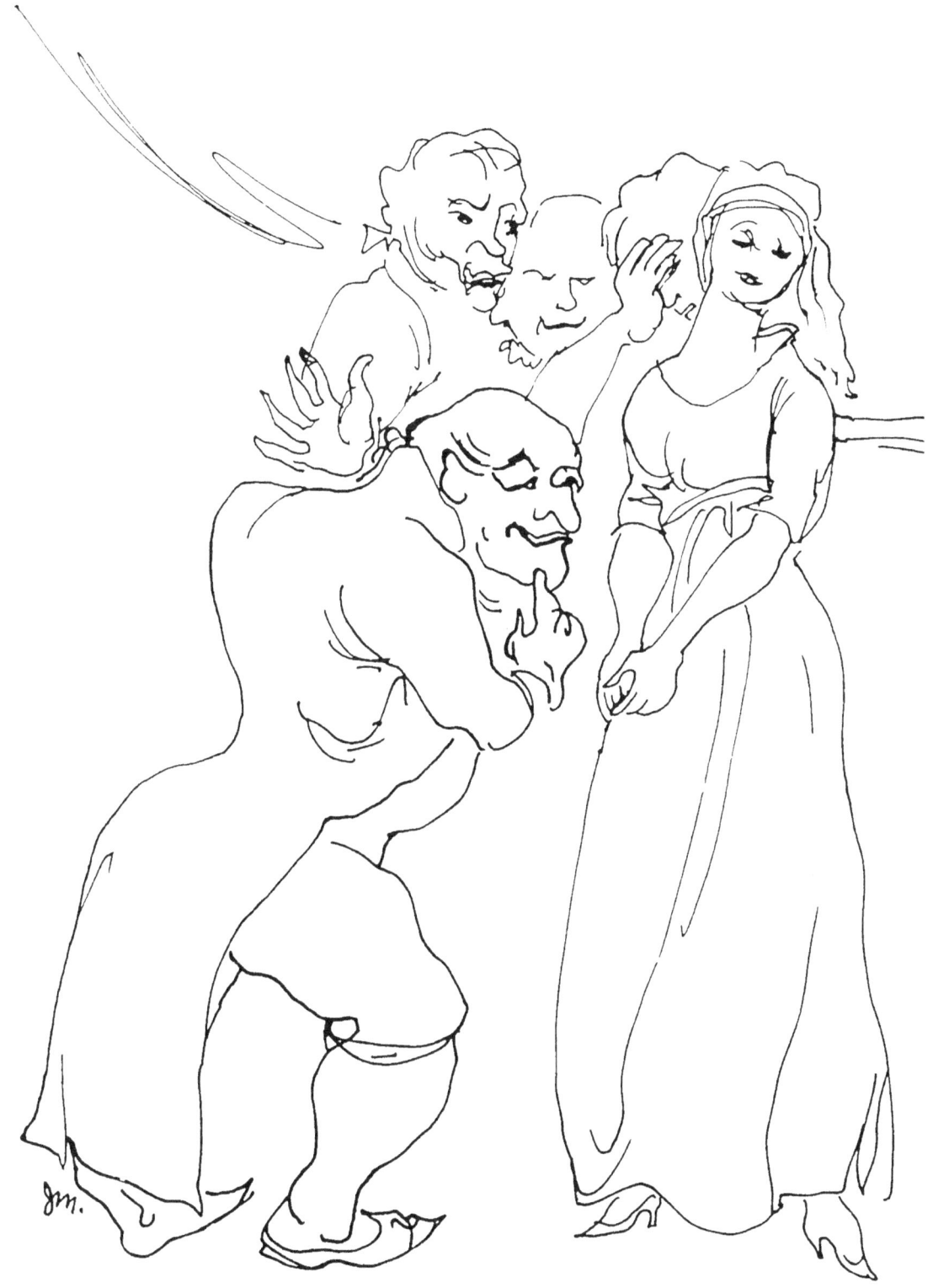

14

What a sacrifice!

15. Nice advice!

Nice advice from a nasty advisor. Too bad the girl will follow it to
the letter. Pity the man who gets anywhere near her!

¡Bellos consejos!

*¡Los consejos son dignos de quien los dá. Lo peor es que la señorita
va ba seguirlos al pie de la letra. Desdichado del que se acerque!*

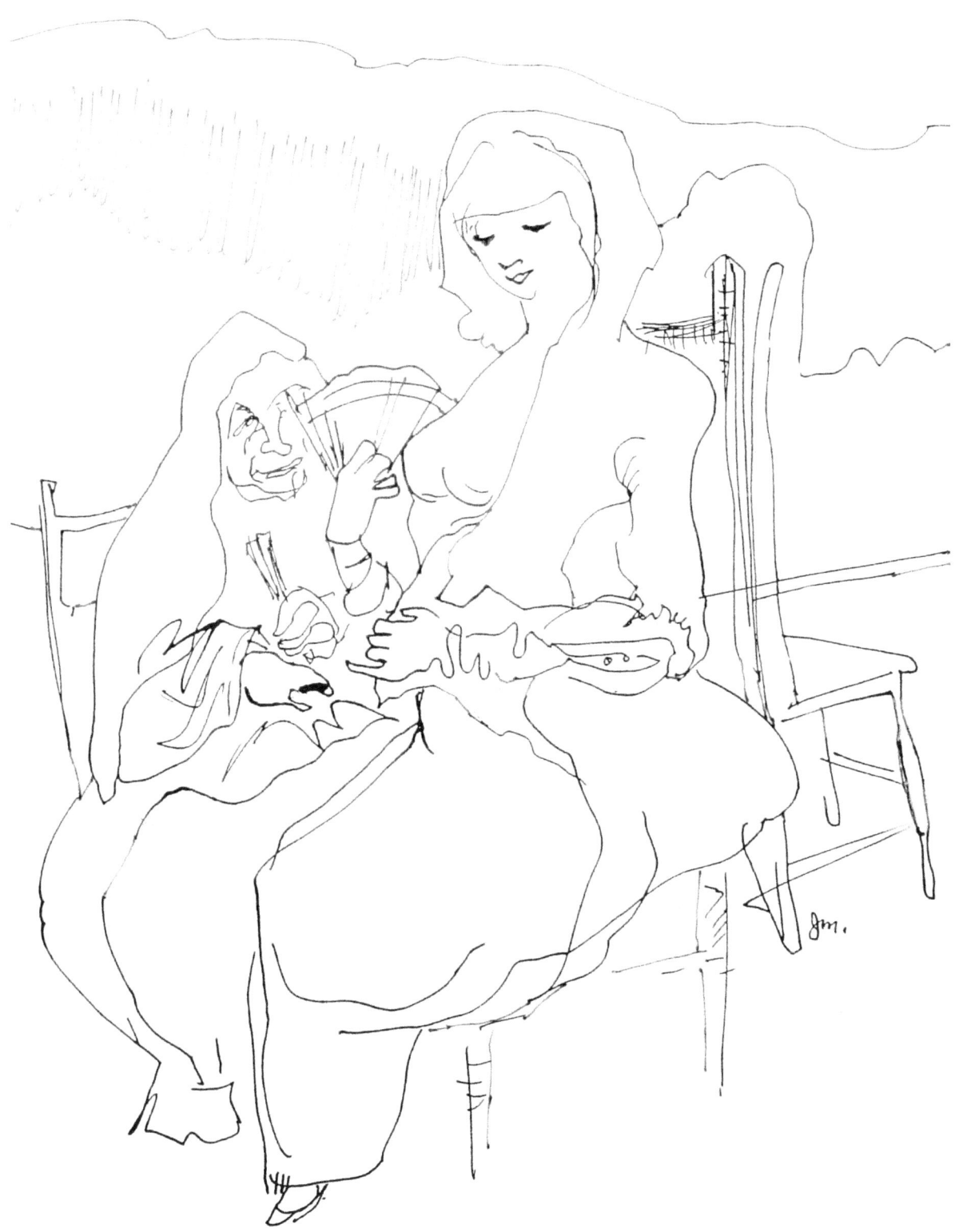

15

Nice advice!

16. It was her mother, for God's sake!

This woman left home as a young innocent. She got educated in Cadiz and came to Madrid where she "won the lottery". She goes to the Prado where she meets, outside, a decrepit, filthy old woman and turns her back on her. The beggar persists until the elegant call girl turns around and finds the poor old woman is her own mother.

¡Dios la perdone: Y era su madre!

La señorita salió muy niña de su tierra: hizo su aprendizaje en Cádiz, vino a Madrid: la cayo la loteria. Baja al Prado, oye que una vieja mugrienta y decrépita la pide limosna, ella la despide ynsta la vieja. Vuélvese la petimetra y halla... ¿quien lo diría?... que la pobretona es su madre.

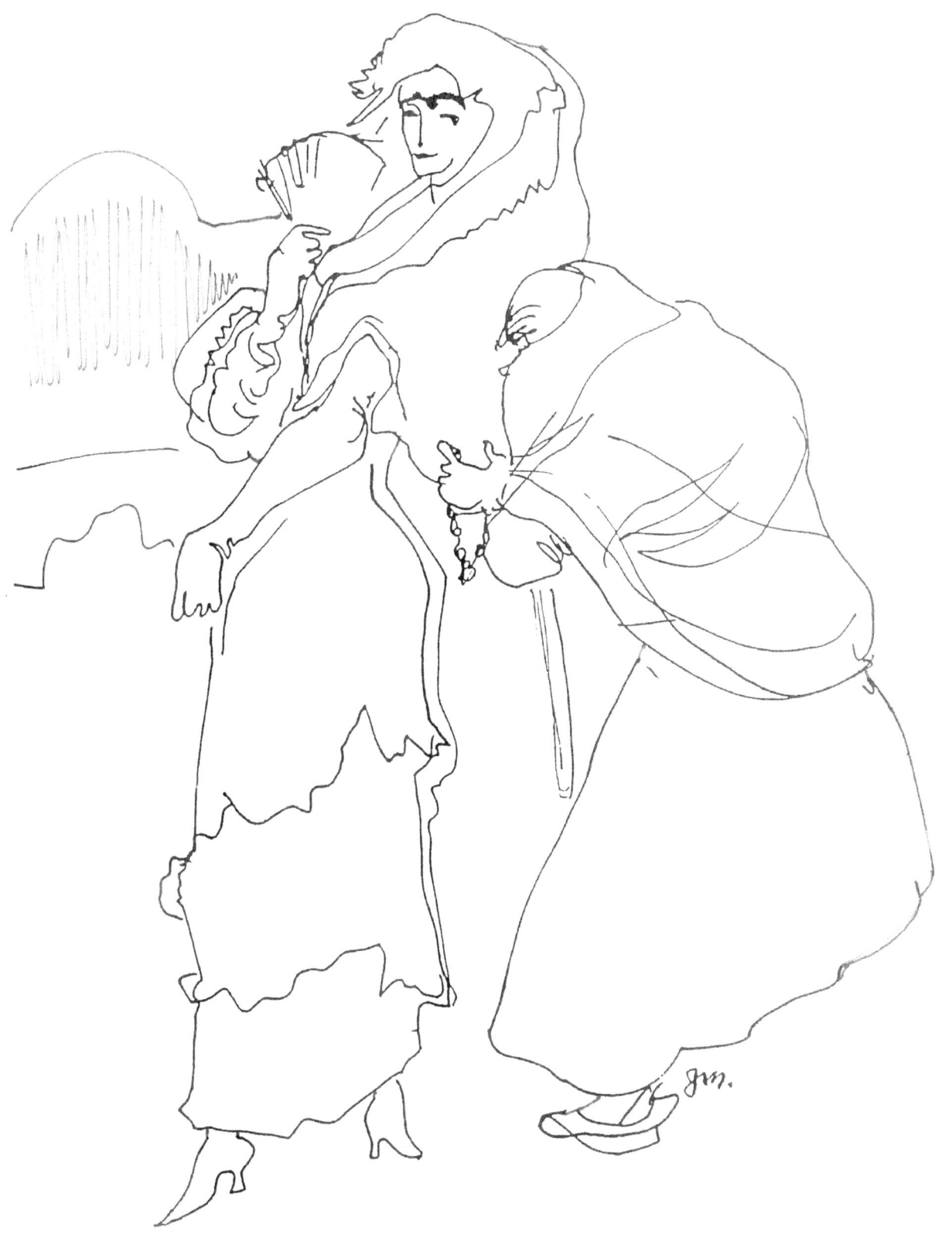

It was her mother, for God's sake!

17. It is nicely stretched.

Oh! The old madam is not stupid. She knows what a call girl needs and that her stockings must be a nice tight fit.

Bien tirade está.

¡Oh! La tía Curra no es tonta. Bien sabe ella lo que conviene que las medias vayan estiraditas.

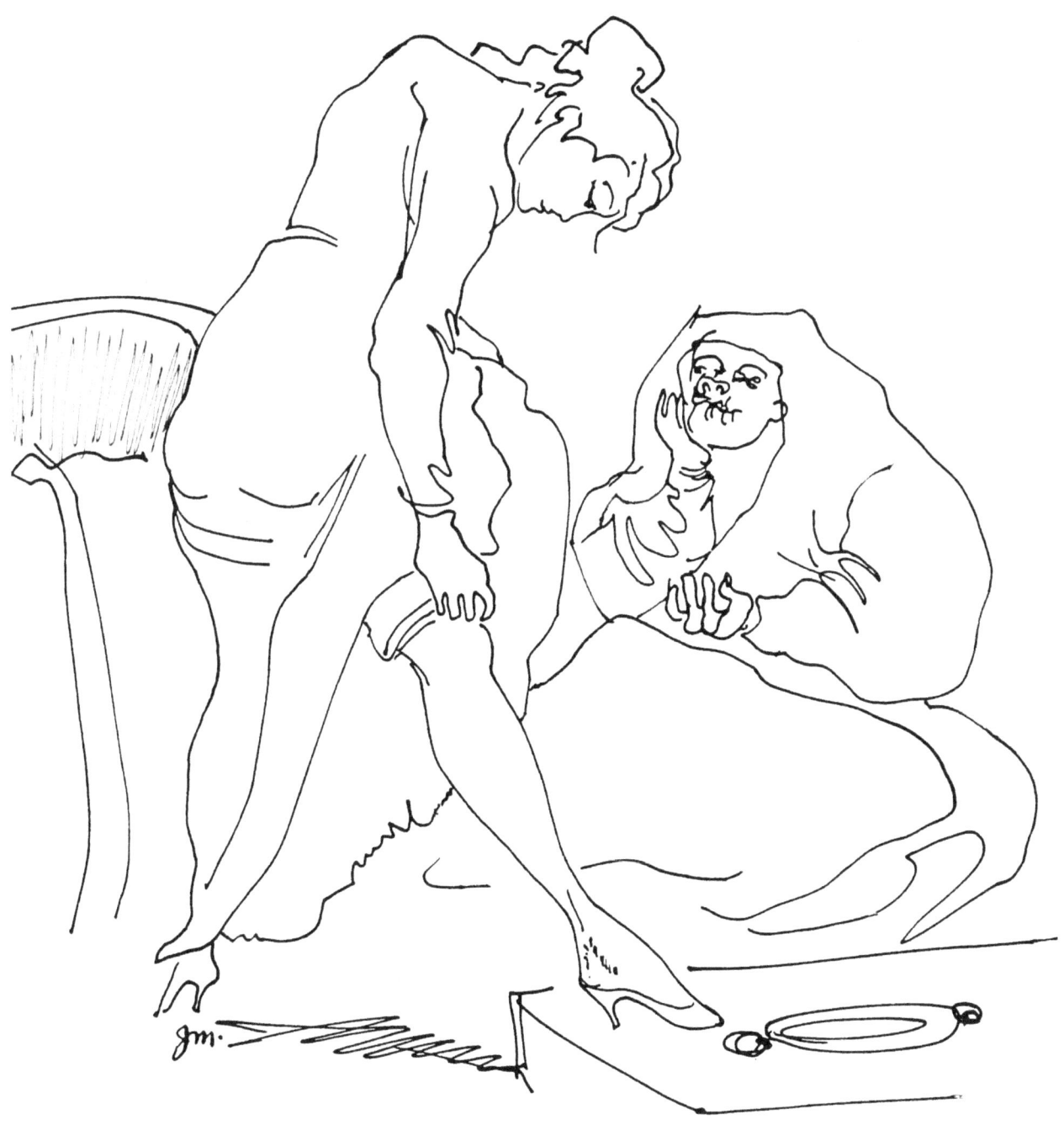

It is nicely stretched.

18. While his house burns!

A result of too much drink.

Y se le quema la casa.

Ní acertara a quitarse los calzones ni dejar de hablar con el candil hasta que las bombas de la villa refresquen. Tanto puede el vino!

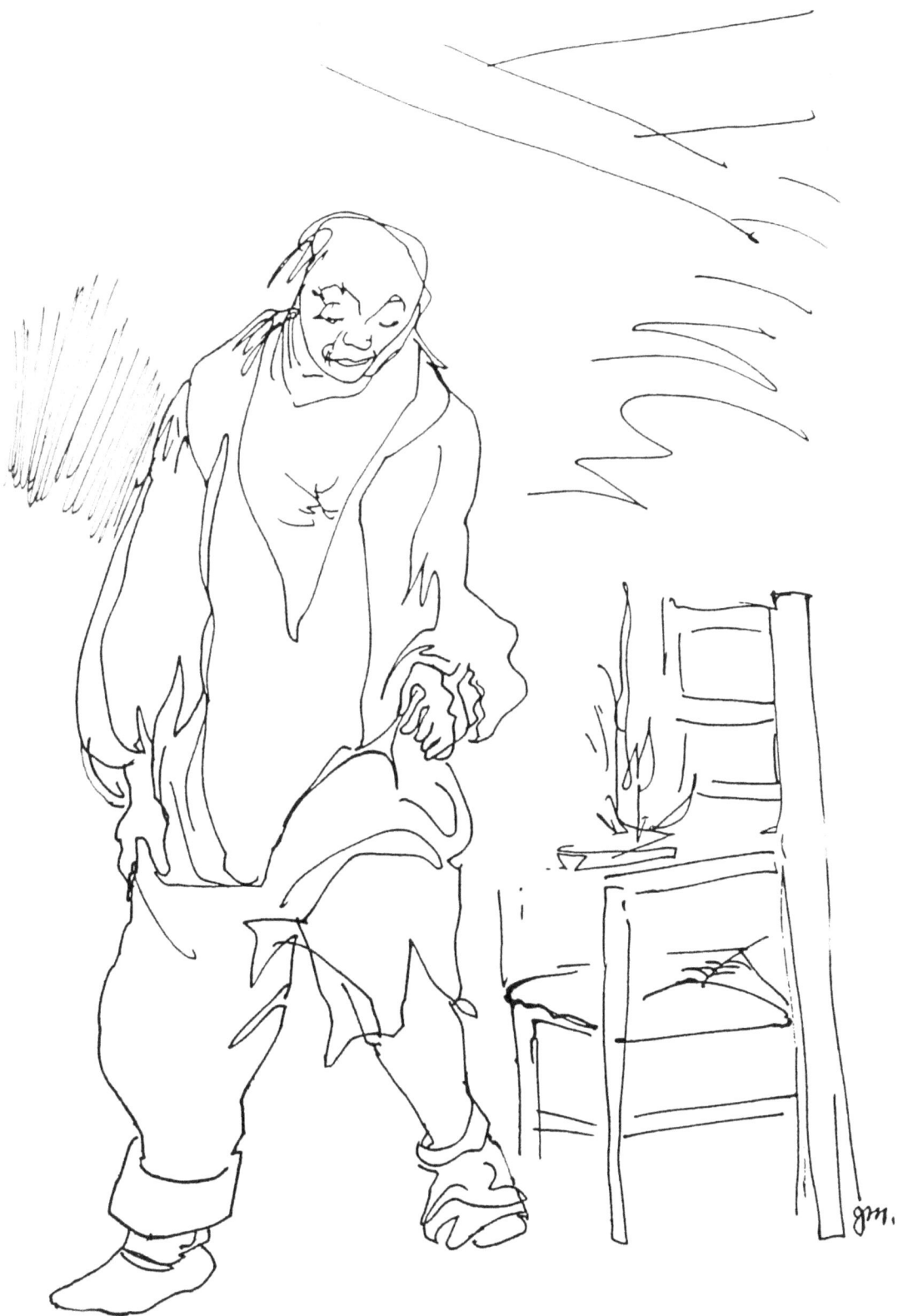

While his house burns.

19. All shall fall.

And those about to fall will not take a warning from those already fallen.
Nothing can be done about it; all shall fall.

Todos caerán.

Y que no escarmienten los que van a caer con el exemplo de los que han caído.
Pero no hay remedio. Todos caerán.

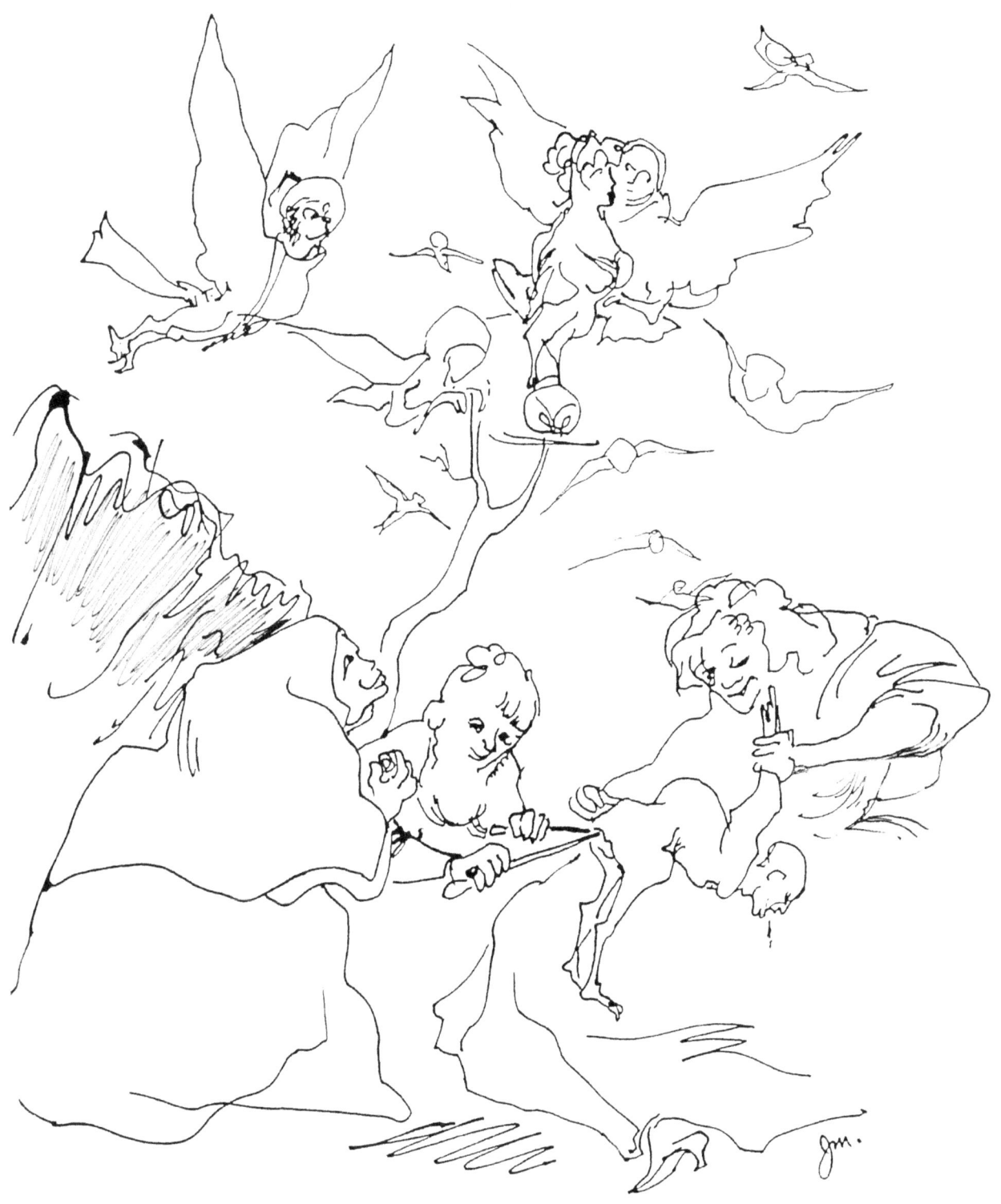

All shall fall.

20. There they go, plucked.

They're done for. Get them out of here and make way for the next guys already on the way.

Ya van desplumados.

Si se desplumaron ya, vayan fuera, que van a venir otros.

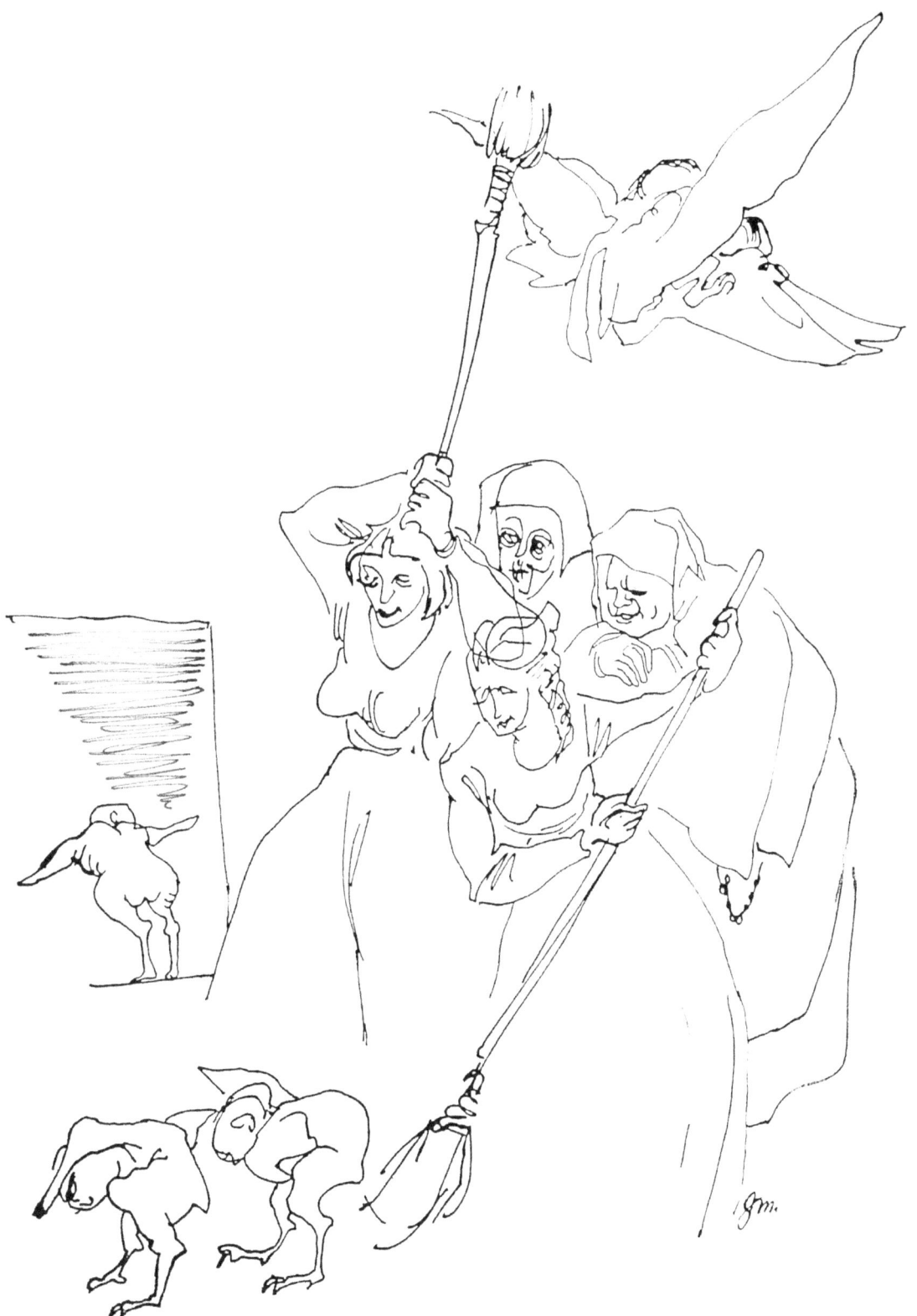

There they go, plucked.

21. How they pluck her!

Chicks also get plucked when they run into predators. So the saying goes: Tit for tat.

¡Qual la descanonan!

Tambien las pollas encuentran milanos que las desplumen y aún por eso se dijo equello de: Donde las dan las toman.

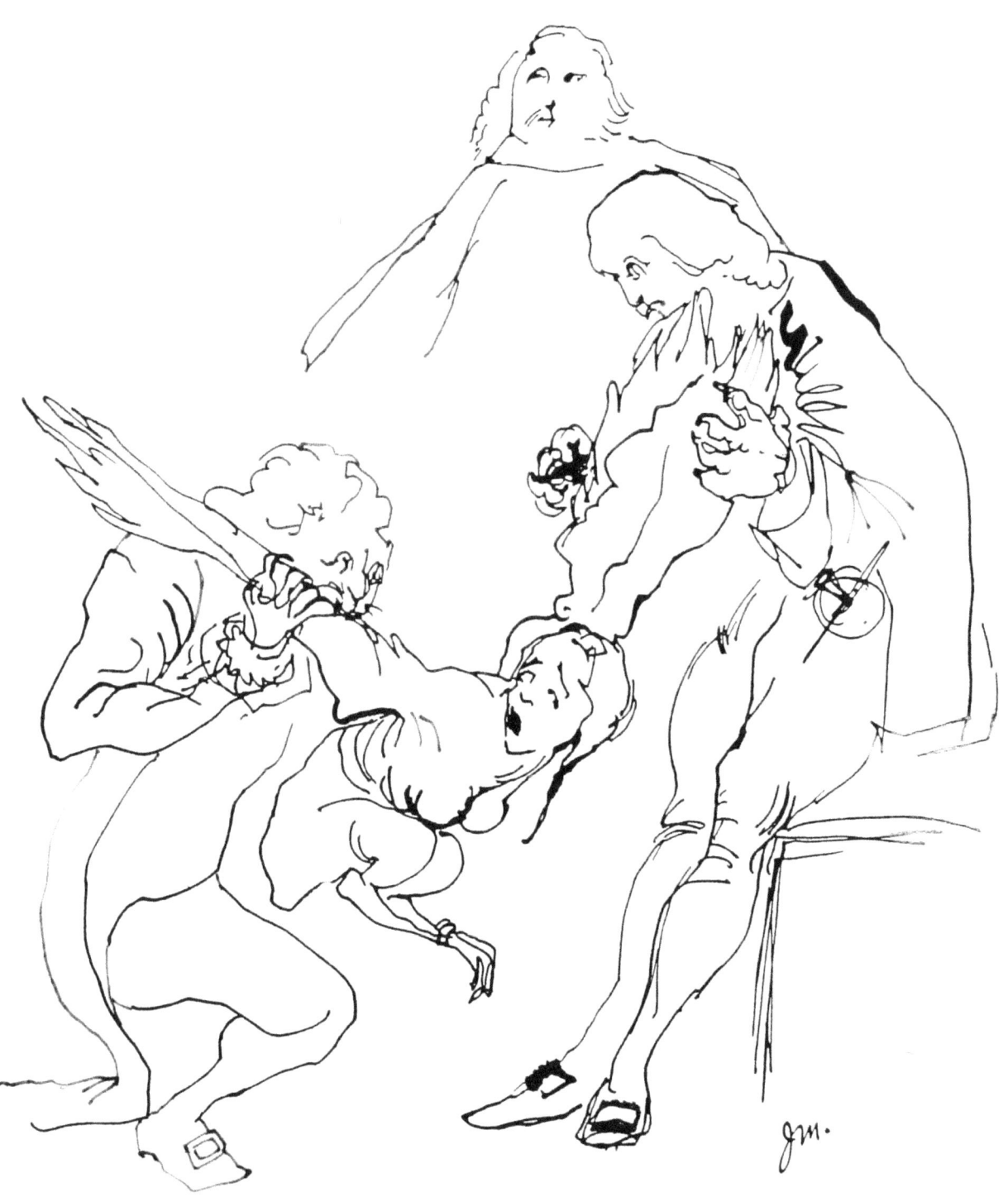

How they pluck her!

22. Poor little things!

They are going to mend these ragamuffins. Take them in, for they have been on the loose long enough.

¡Pobrecitas!

Vayan a coser las descosidas. Recojánlas que bastante anduvieron sueltas.

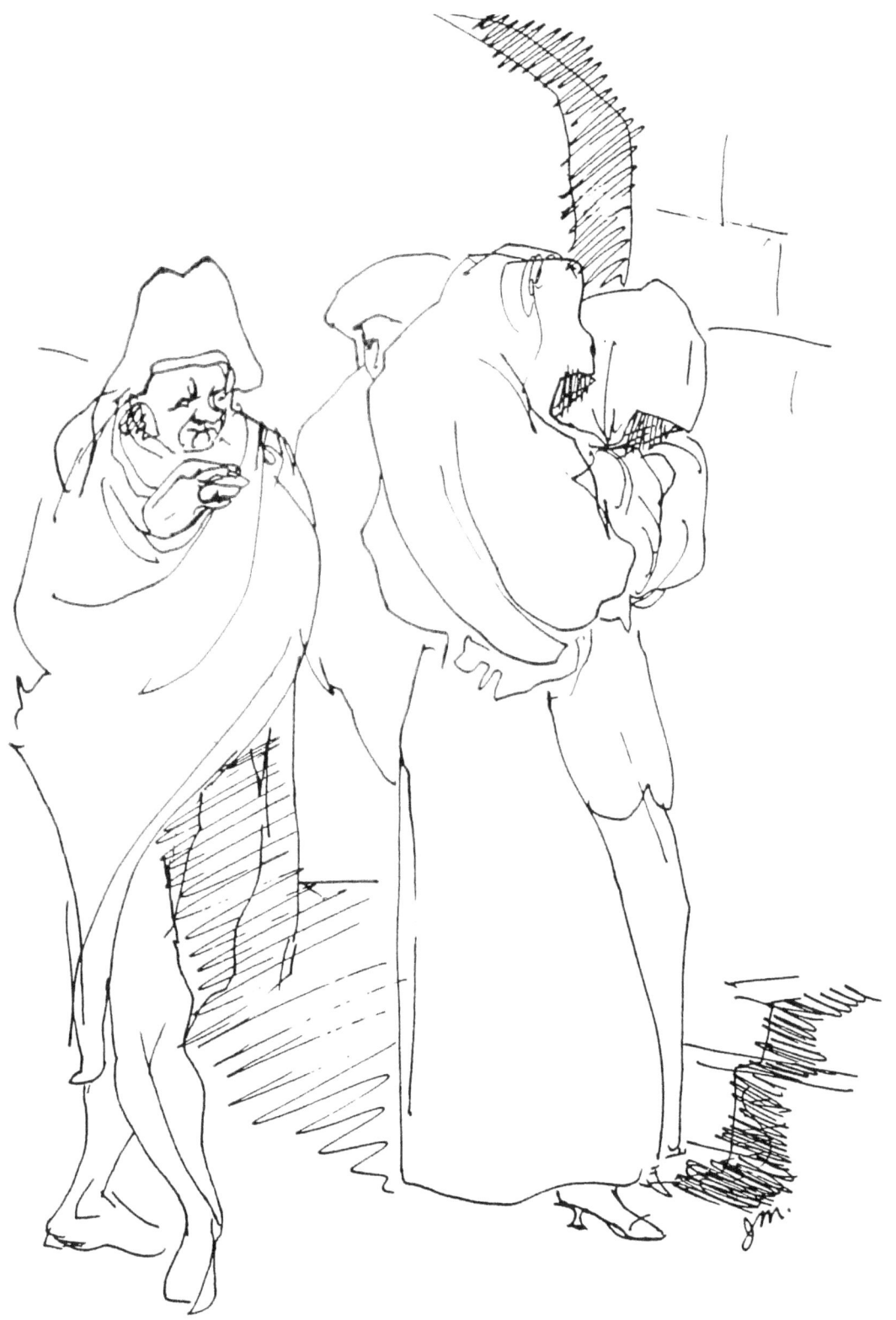

Poor little things!

23. For shame!

To catch in the Inquistion an honorable woman who served the world so diligently, so usefully, just for a crust of bread. What a shame!

Aquellos polbos.

Mal hecho! A una mujer de onor, que por una friolera servía a todo el mundo, tan dilijente, tan útil, tratarla asi. Mal hecho!

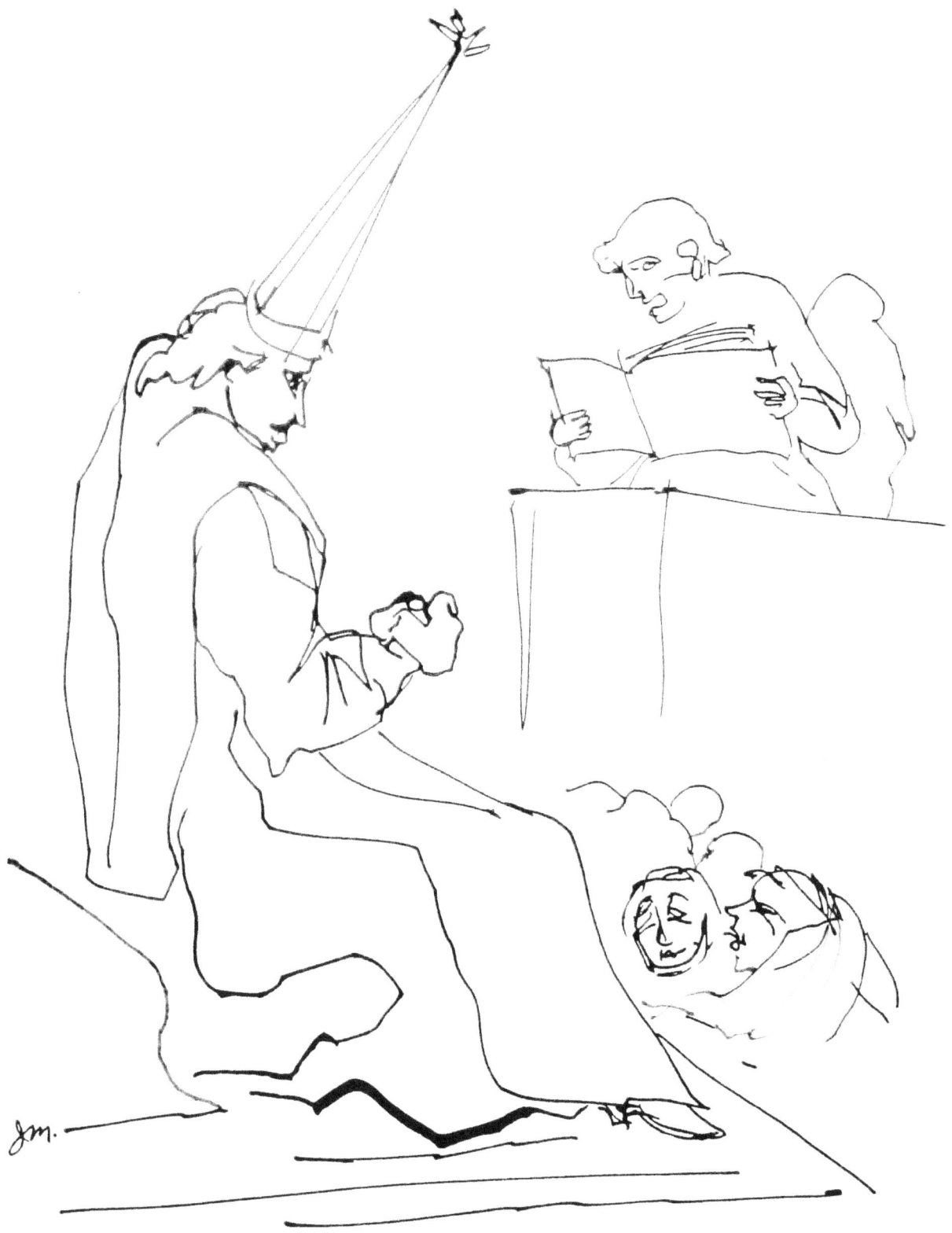

23

For shame!

24. There was no help for it.

This sainted lady is being persecuted to death. If they take her out in triumph to shame her they are wasting their time. Nobody can shame one who knows no shame.

No hubo remedio.

A esta Sta. Señora la persiquien de muerte!: después de escrivirla la vida la sacan en triunfo. Todo se lo merece y si lo hacen por afrentarla es tiempo perdido. Nadie puede abergonzar a quien no tiene bergüenza.

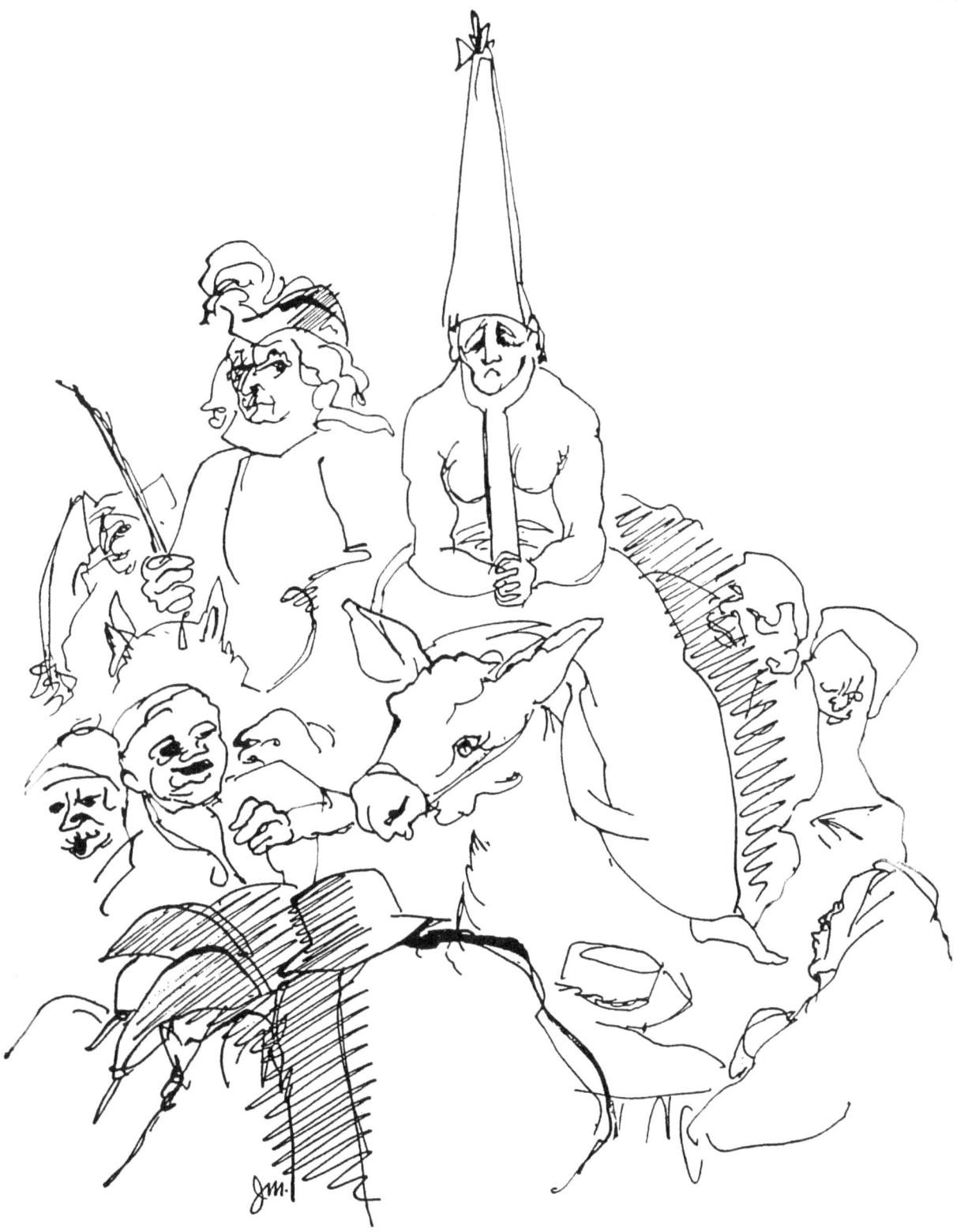

There was no help for it.

25. Sure, he broke the pot.
The kid is a mischief maker and the mother is mean. Who is worse?

Si quebró el Cántaro.
El hijo es travieso y la madre es colérica. Quál es peor?

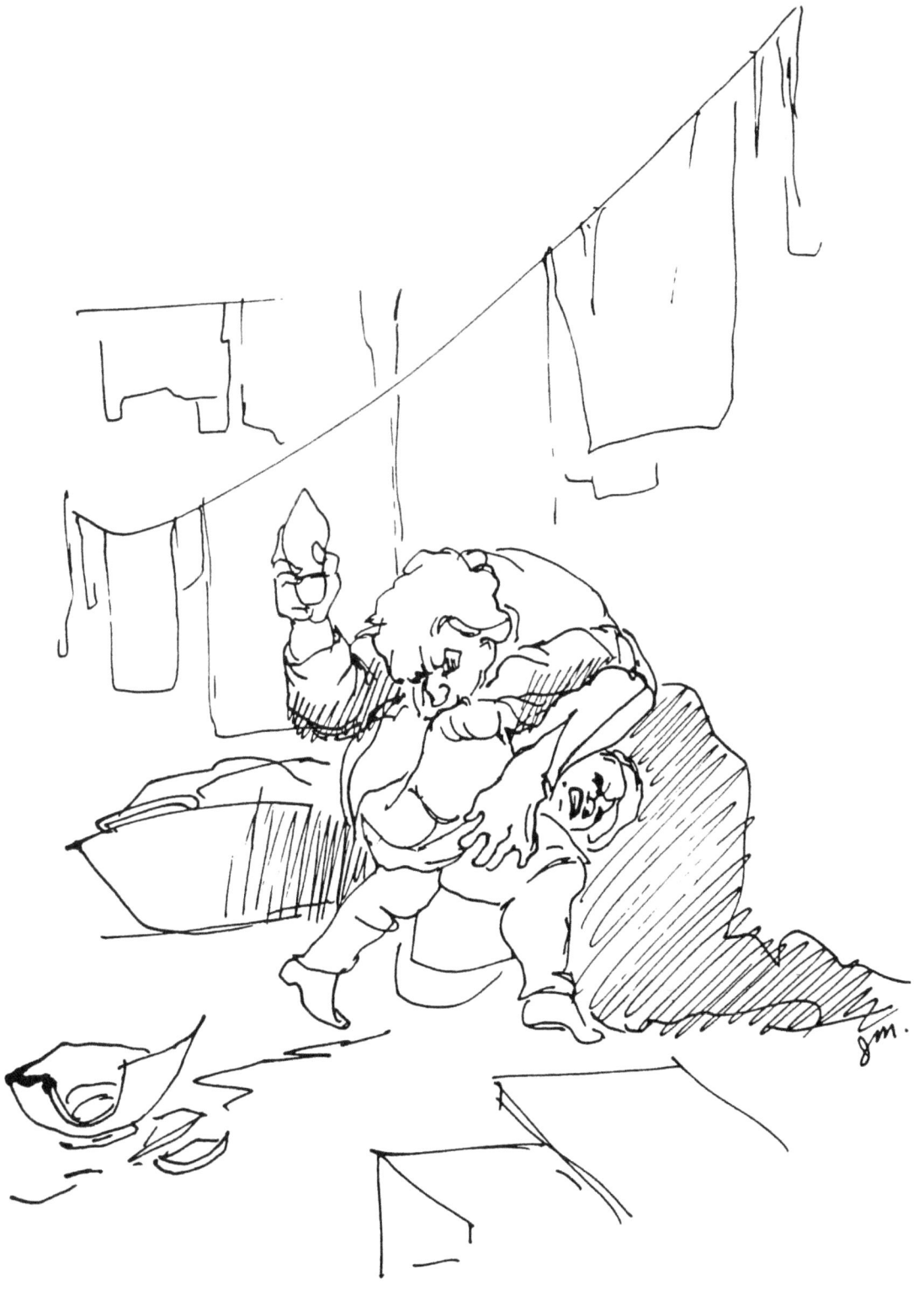

Sure, he broke the pot.

26. They have plenty to sit on.

If they're conceited about their bottoms there's nothing better than to put their seats on their heads.

Ya tienen asiento.

Para que las niñas casquibanas tengan asiento no hay mejor cosa que ponérselo en la cabeza.

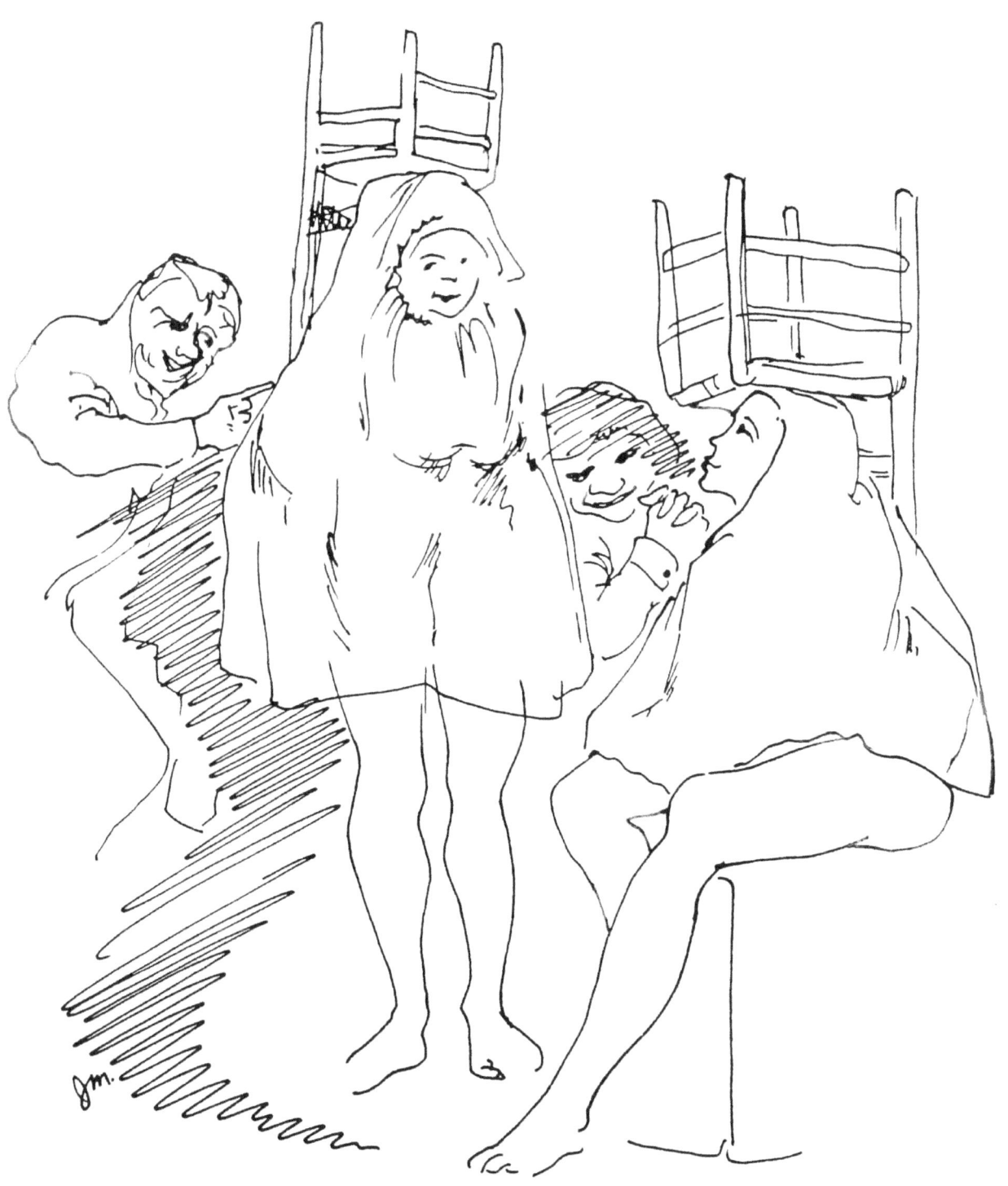

They have plenty to sit on.

27. Which of them is the most overcome?

Neither the one not the other. He is a two-faced liar who tells all the girls the same thing. She is wondering how she can keep the five appointments she made between 8:00 and 9:00 when it is already 7:30.

¿Quien mas rendido?

Ni uno ni otro! El es un charlatán de amor que a todas dice lo mismo y ella está pensando en evacuar 5 citas que tiene dadas entre 8 y 9 y son las 7 y 1/2.

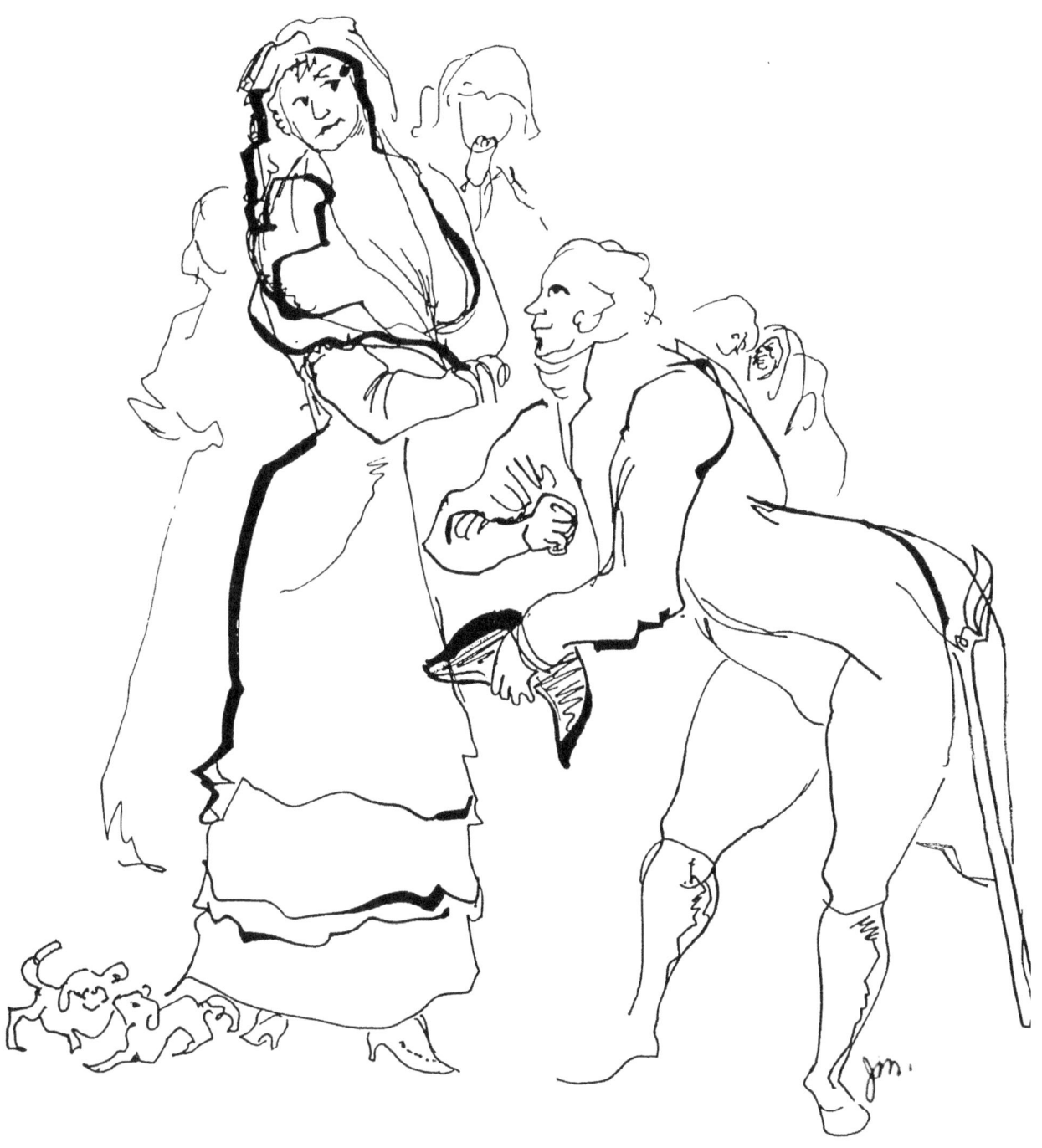

Which of them is the most overcome?

28. Shh!

A fine mother to trust with a secret.

¡Chiton!

Excelente madre para un encargo de confianza.

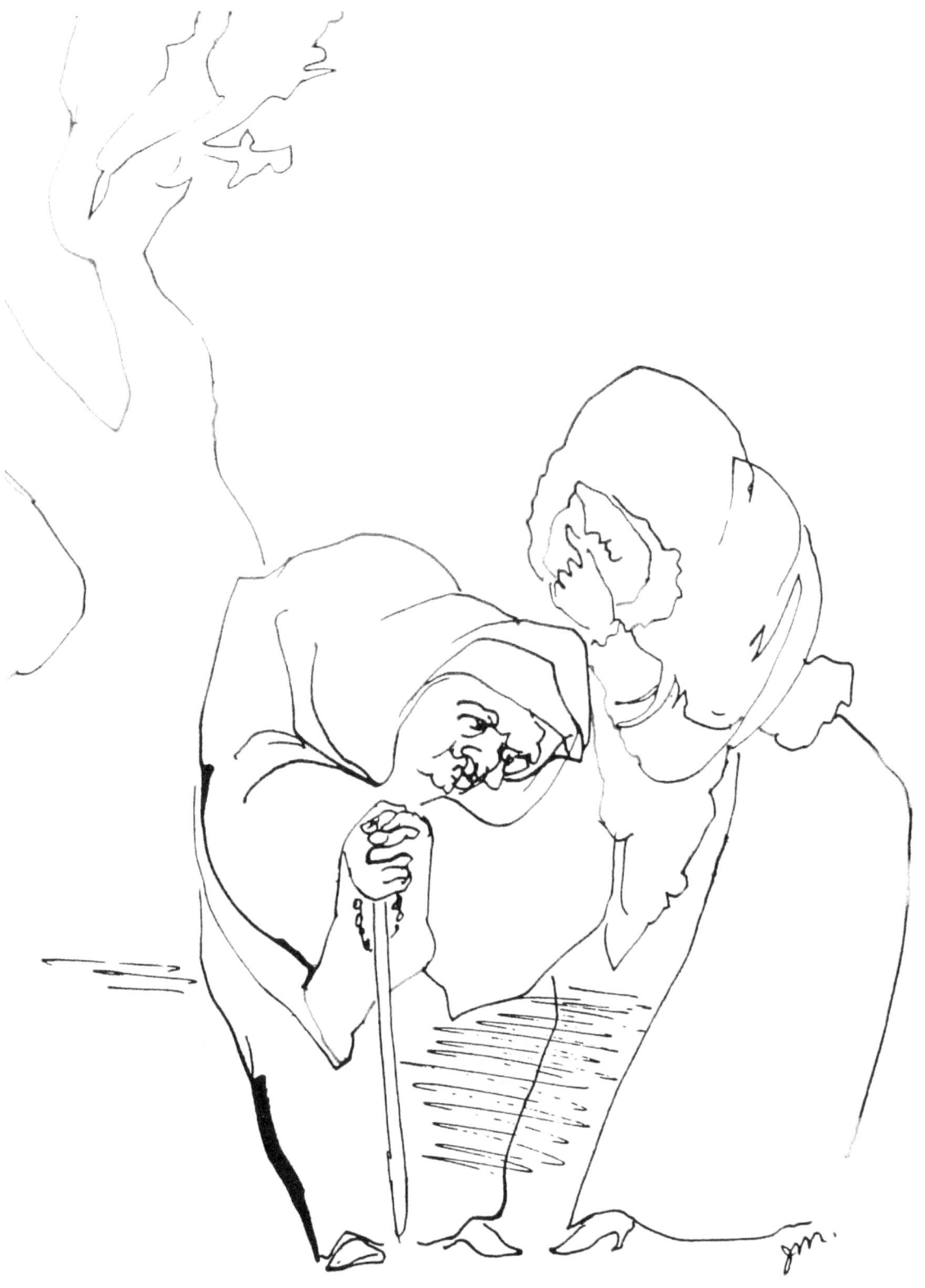

Shh!

29. He is certainly reading.

They comb his hair, they put on his shoes while he studies; but he is sleeping. No one can accuse him of wasting his time.

Esto si que es leer.

Le pienan, le calzan, duerme y estudia. Nadie dirá que desaprobecha el tiempo.

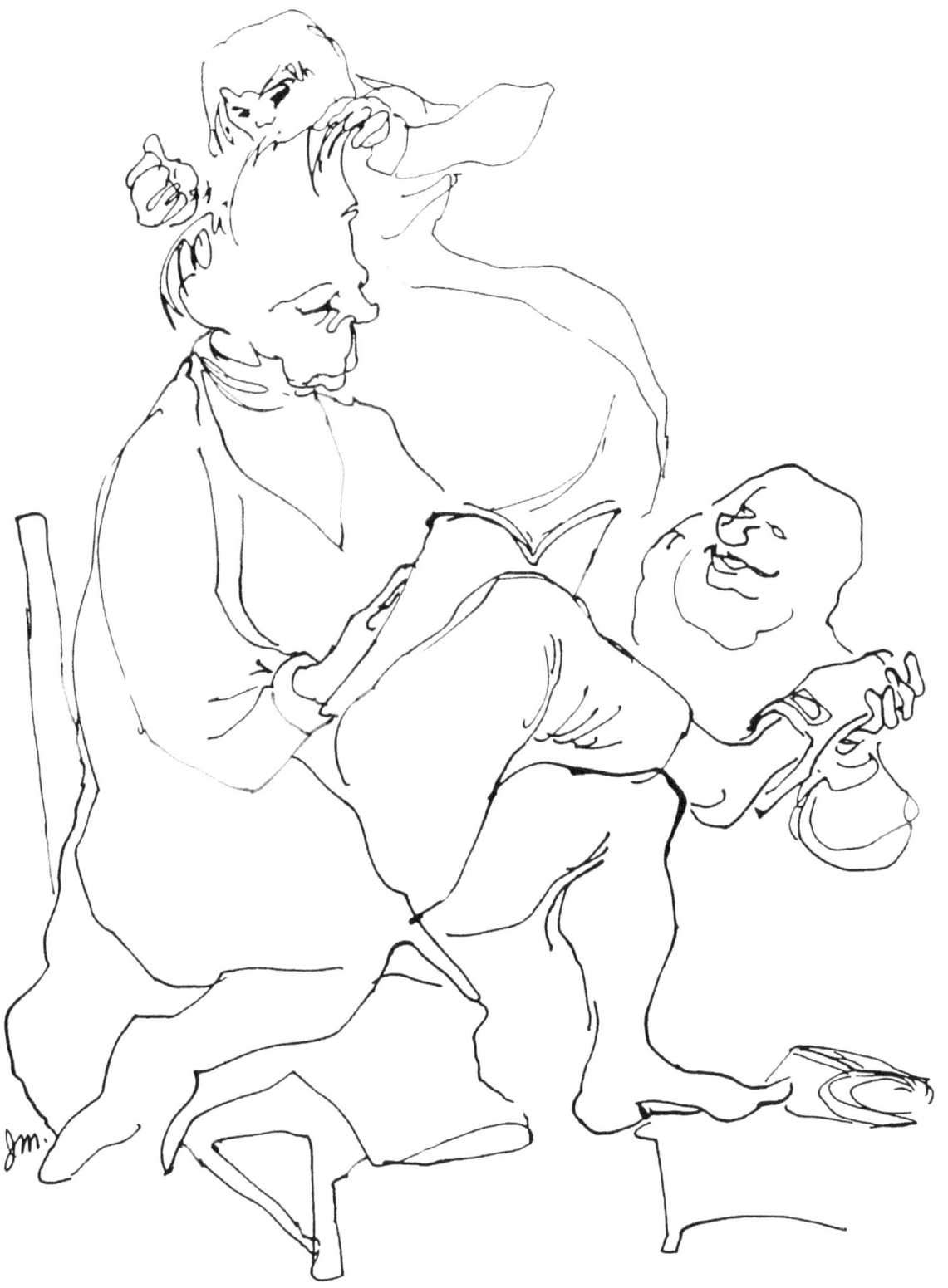

He is certainly reading.

30. Why keep hiding them?

He hides his treasures because he thinks he is going to live long enough to be in want, even though he's over 80 and he'll die next month. Greed doesn't calculate correctly.

¿Porque esconderlos?

La respuesta es fácil. Porque no los quiere gastar, y no los gasta porque aunque tiene los 80 cumplidos y no puede vivir un mes todavía, teme que le ha de sobrar la vida y faltarle el dinero. Tan equibocados son los cálculos de la avaricia.

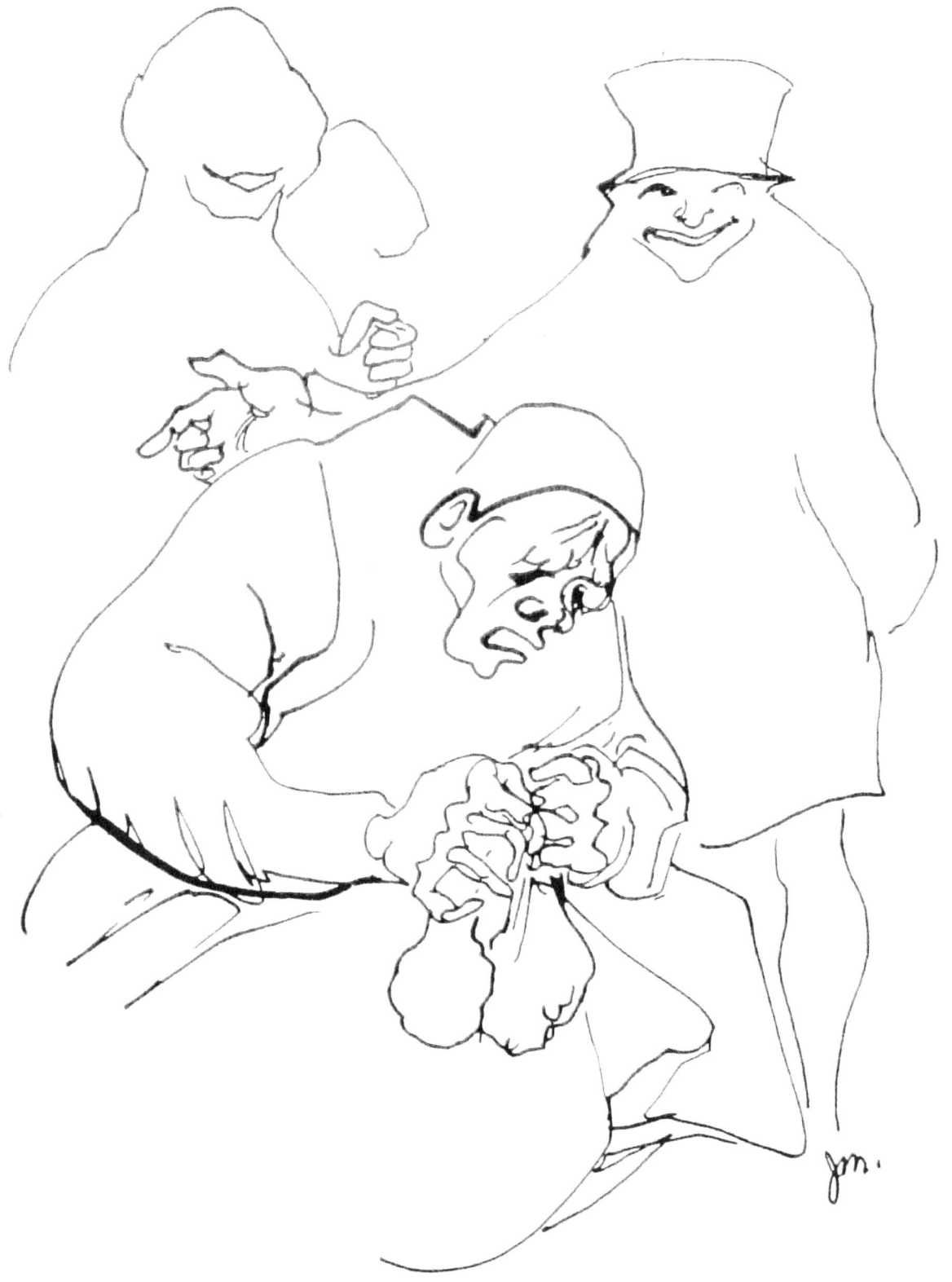

30

Why keep hiding them?

31. She prays for her.

As well she might; may God send her luck, keep her from harm
and from doctors and cops and make her as willing and lively
and eager as her mother who is in heaven.

Ruega por ella.

*Y hace muy bien, para que Dios la de fortuna y la libre de mal
y de cirujanos y alguaciles y llegue a ser tan diestra, tan despejada y tan
para todo como su madre, que en gloria esté.*

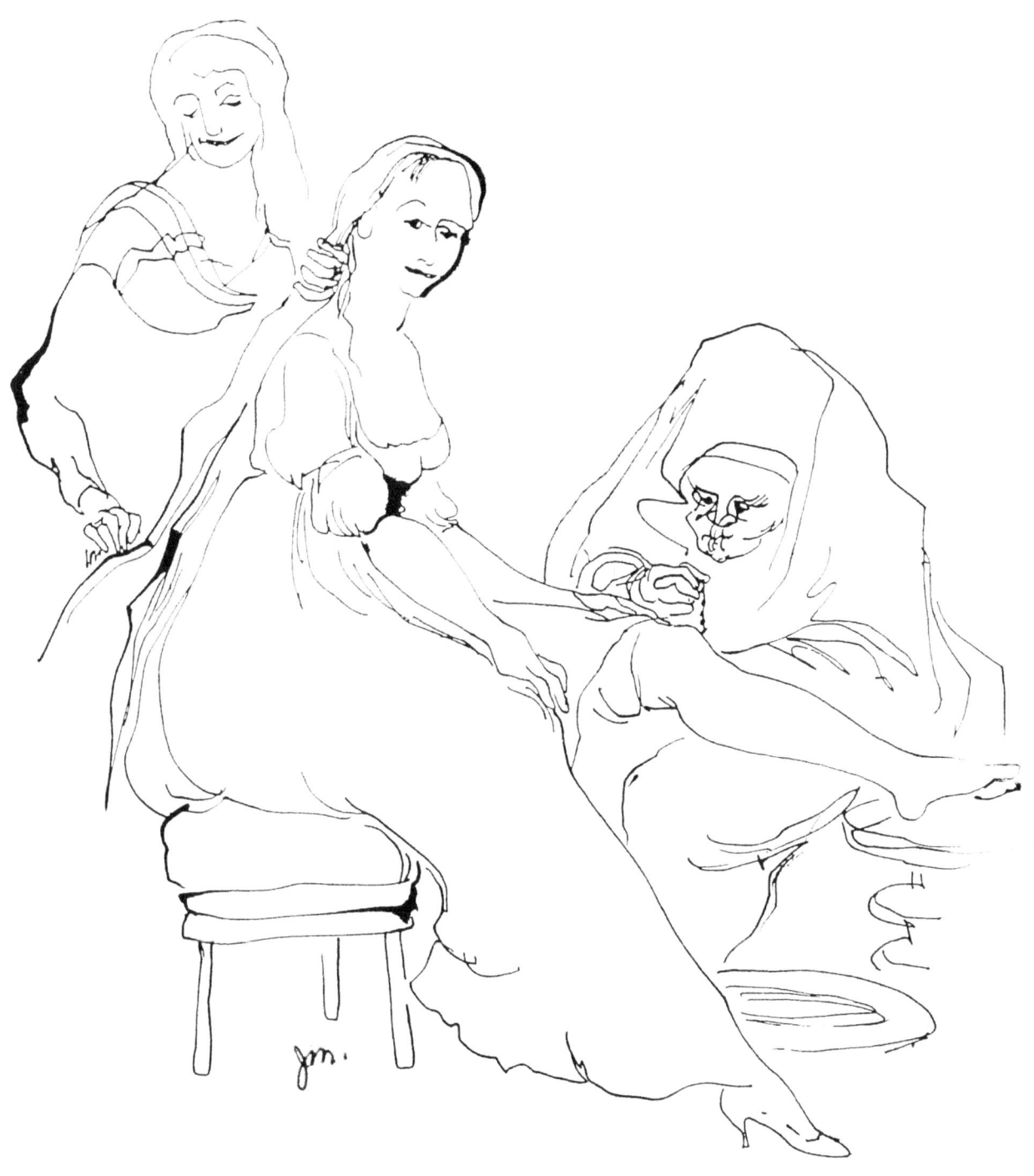

31

She prays for her.

32. Because she was sensitive.

It was bound to happen in this world with its ups and downs. She was
leading a life that was guaranteed to end like this.

Por que fue sensible.

*Cómo ha de ser; este mundo tiene sus altos y bajos. La vida que ella tra hía
no podía parar en otra cosa.*

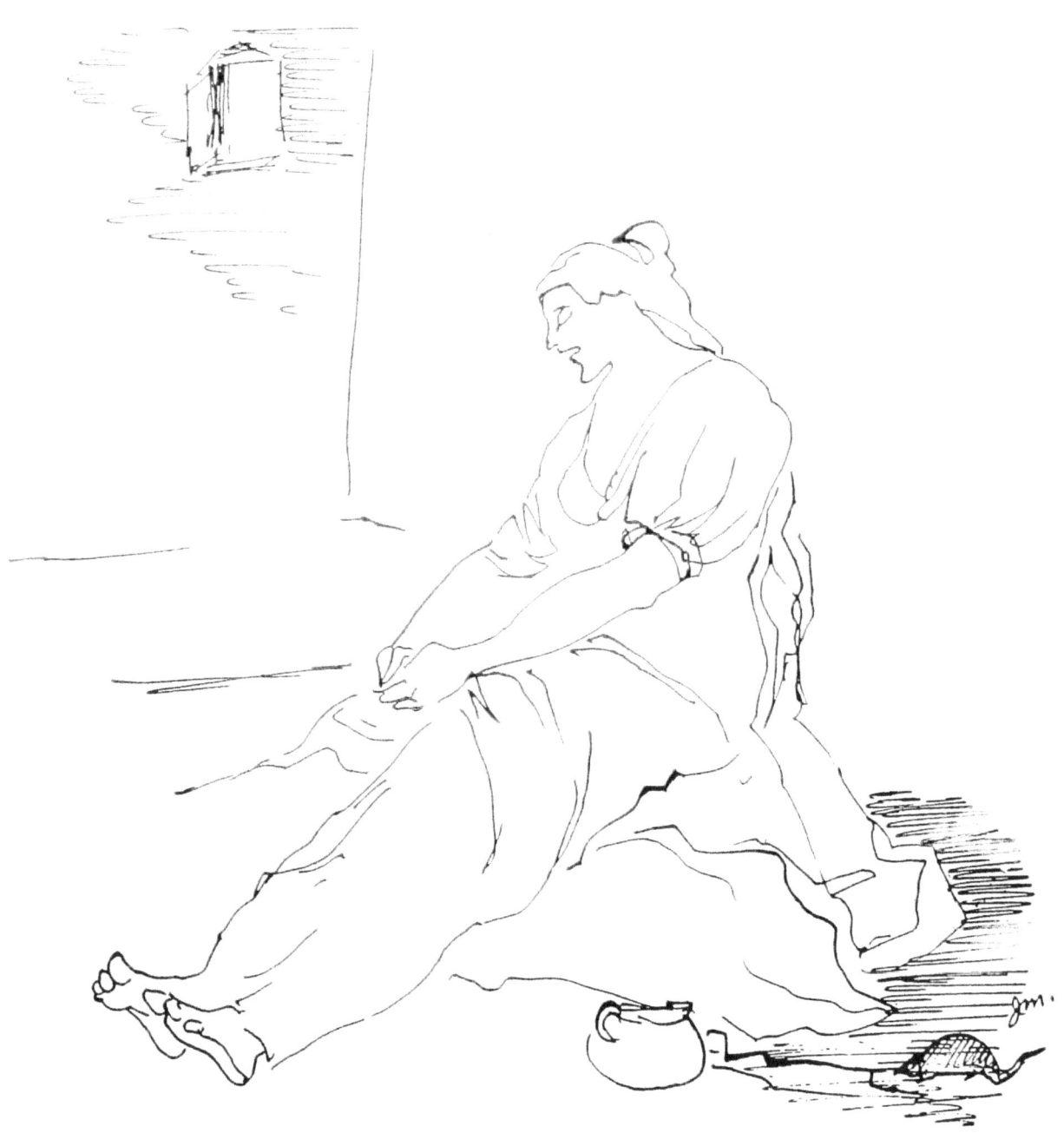

32

Because she was sensitive.

33. To The Count Palatine.

Every science is full of quacks who know everything without studying anything and have a remedy for every problem. Don't trust one word they say. A really wise man is cautious about making predictions. He promises little but accomplishes a lot; but the Count Palatine promises everything and produces nothing.

Al Conde Palatino.

En todas ciencias hay charlatans que sin haber estudiado palabra lo saben todo y para todo hallan remedio. No hay que fiarse de lo que anuncian. El verdadero sabio desconfía siempre del acierto; promete poco y cumple mucho; pero el Conde Palatino, no cumple nada de lo que promete.

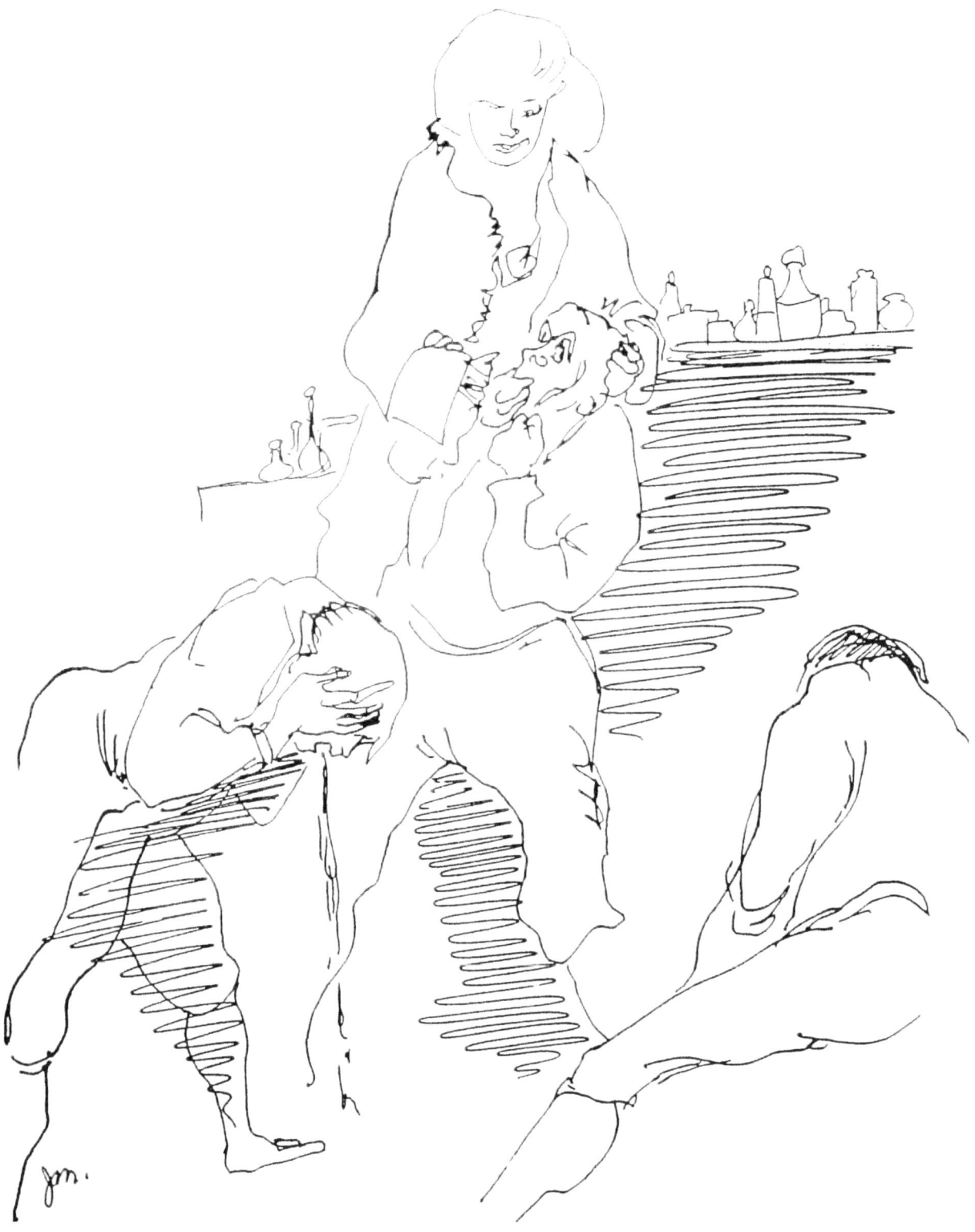

To The Count Palatine.

34. Fast asleep!

Don't wake them up. Sometimes sleep is the only happiness of those who are miserable.

Las rinde el sueño.

No hay que dispertarlas, tal vez el sueño es la única felicidad de los desdichados.

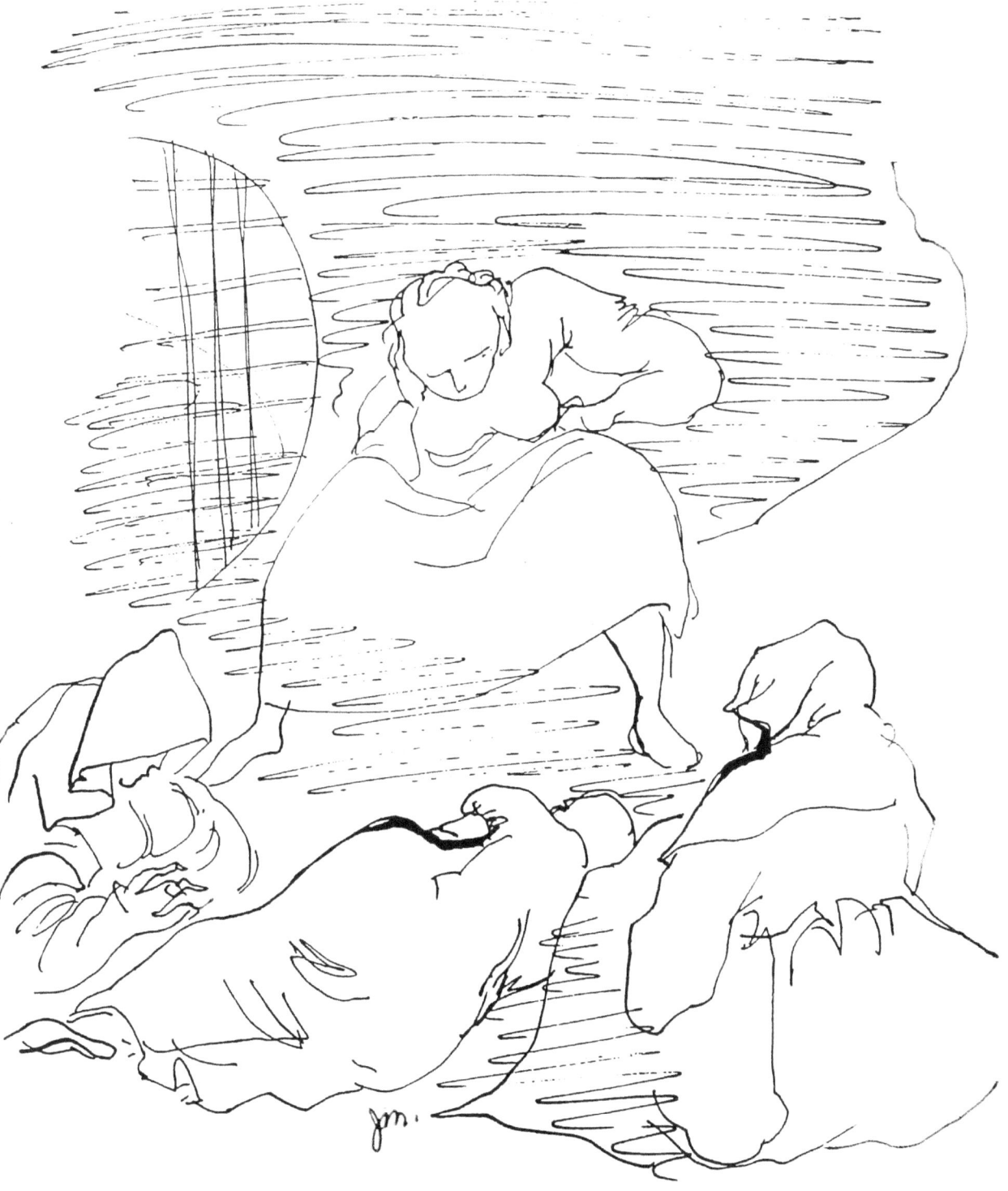

Fast asleep!

35. A close shave!

They give him a close shave and fleece him. But he asked for it when he went to the owner of such a clip joint.

¡Le descañona!

Le descañonan y le desollaran. La culpa tiene quien se pone en manos de tal barbero.

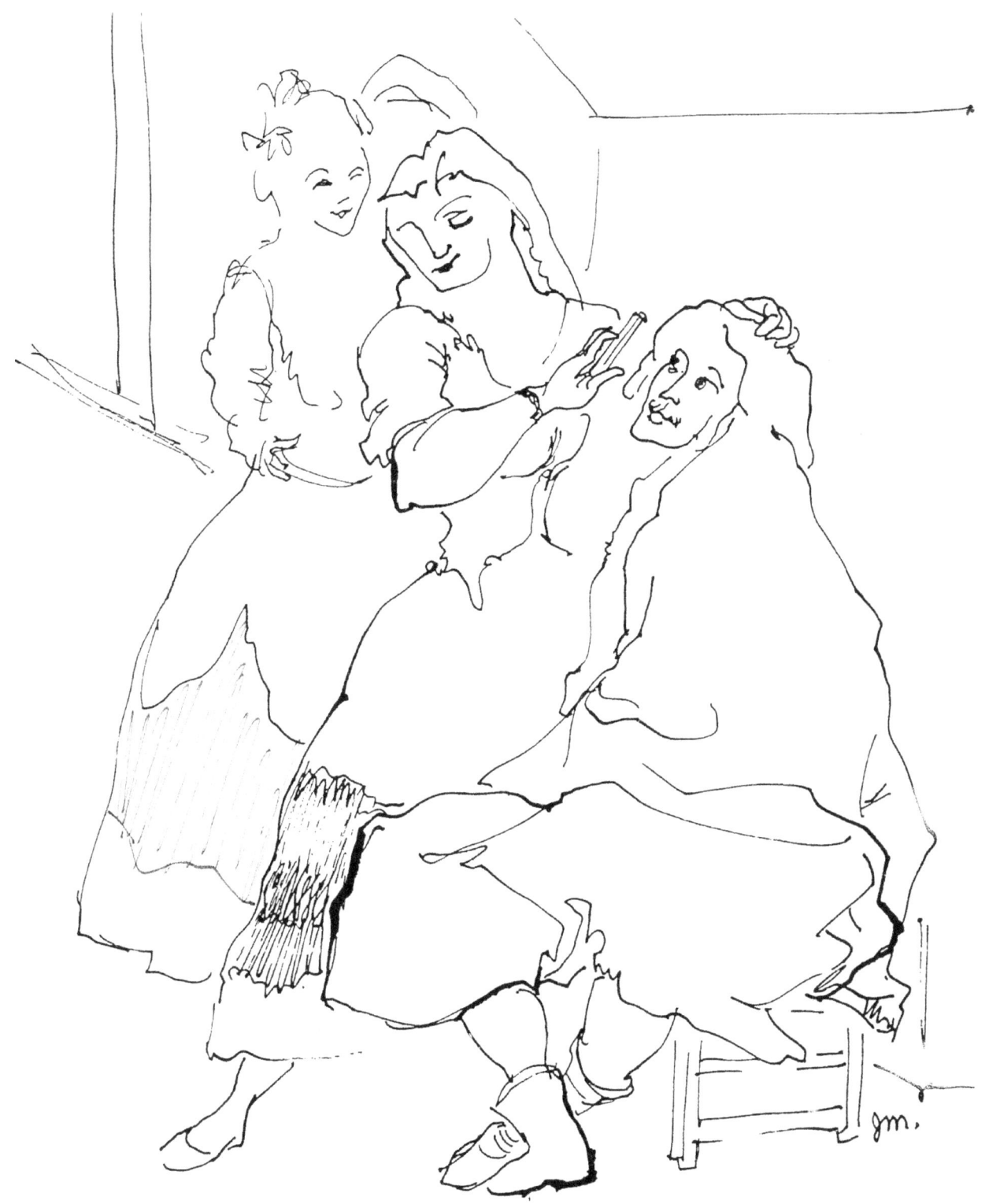

A close shave!

36. An evil night.
This is what happens to alley cat girls who won't stay home.

Mala noche.
A esto trabajos se esponen las niñas pindongas que no se quieren estar en casa.

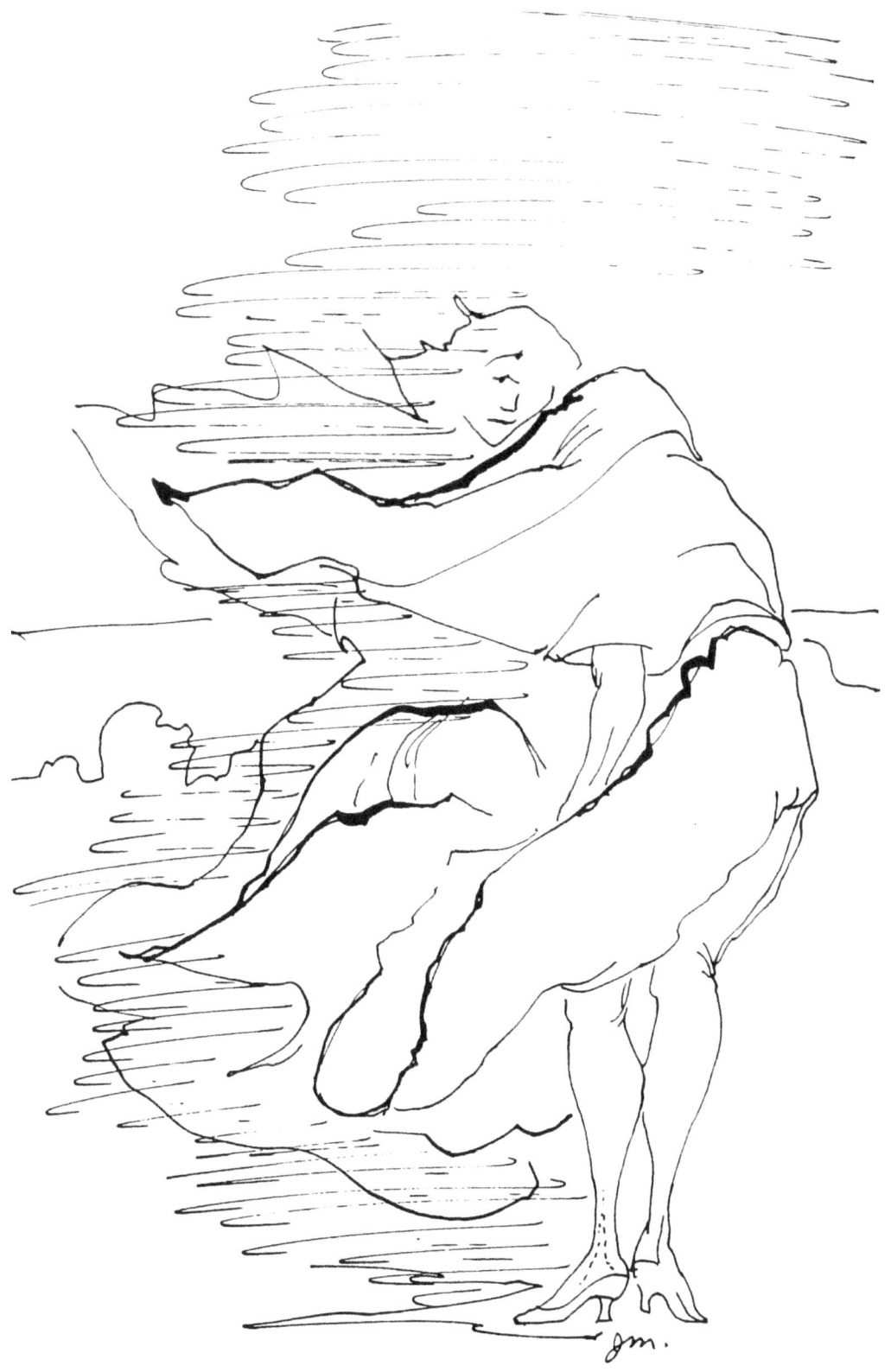

An evil night.

37. What if the pupil knows more?

Who can tell if he knows more or less. What's certain is that the teacher is the most serious looking person around.

¿Si sabrá mas el discípulo?

No se sabe si sabrá más o menos, lo cierto es que el maestro es el personaje más grabe que se ha podido encontrar.

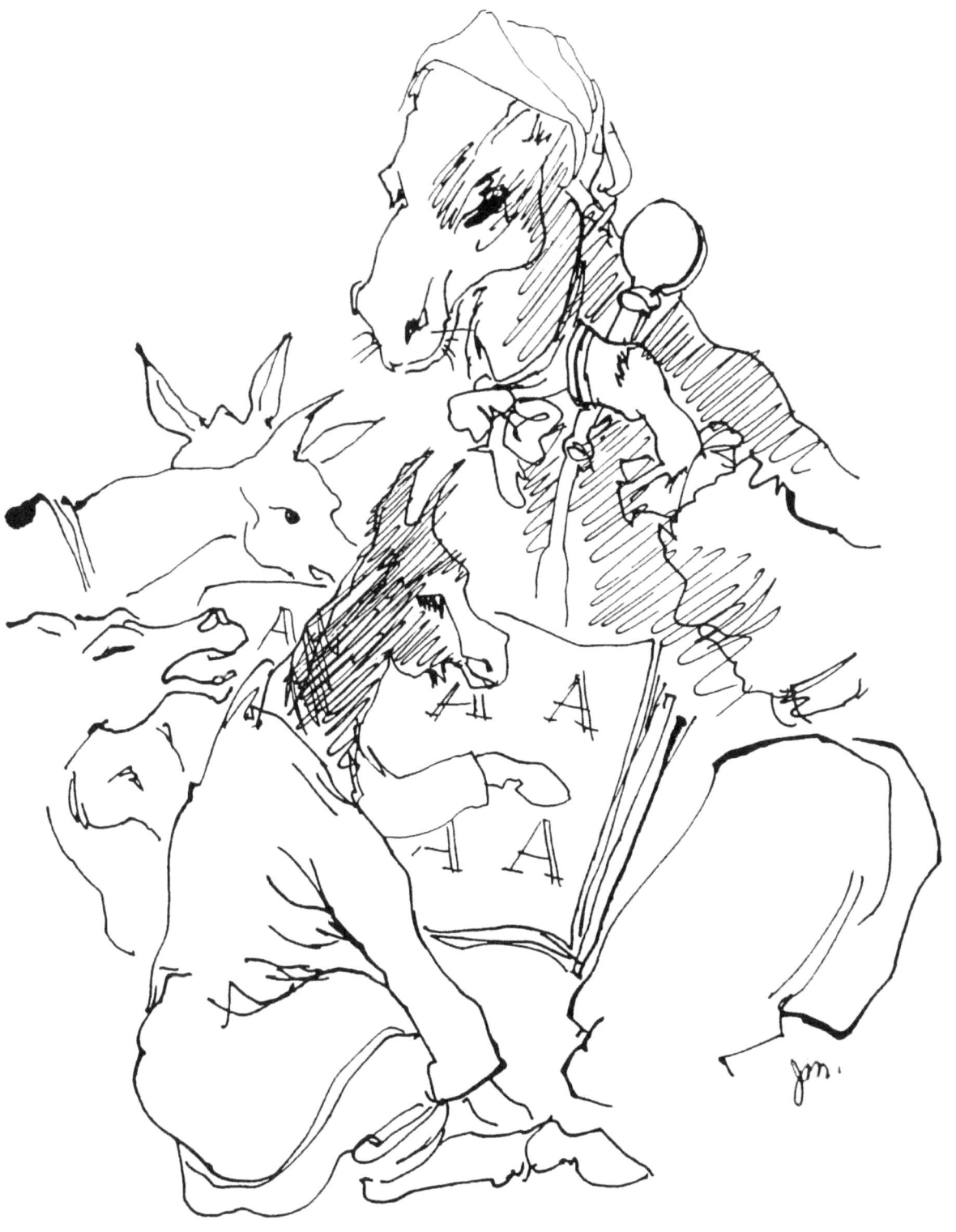

37

What if the pupil knows more?

38. Bravo!

If nothing was needed but ears to appreciate music, no one could be a better listener. But he's applauding what isn't being played.

¡Brabisimo!

Si para entenderlo bastan las orejas nadie habrá más intelligente;
pero es de temer que aplauda lo que no suena.

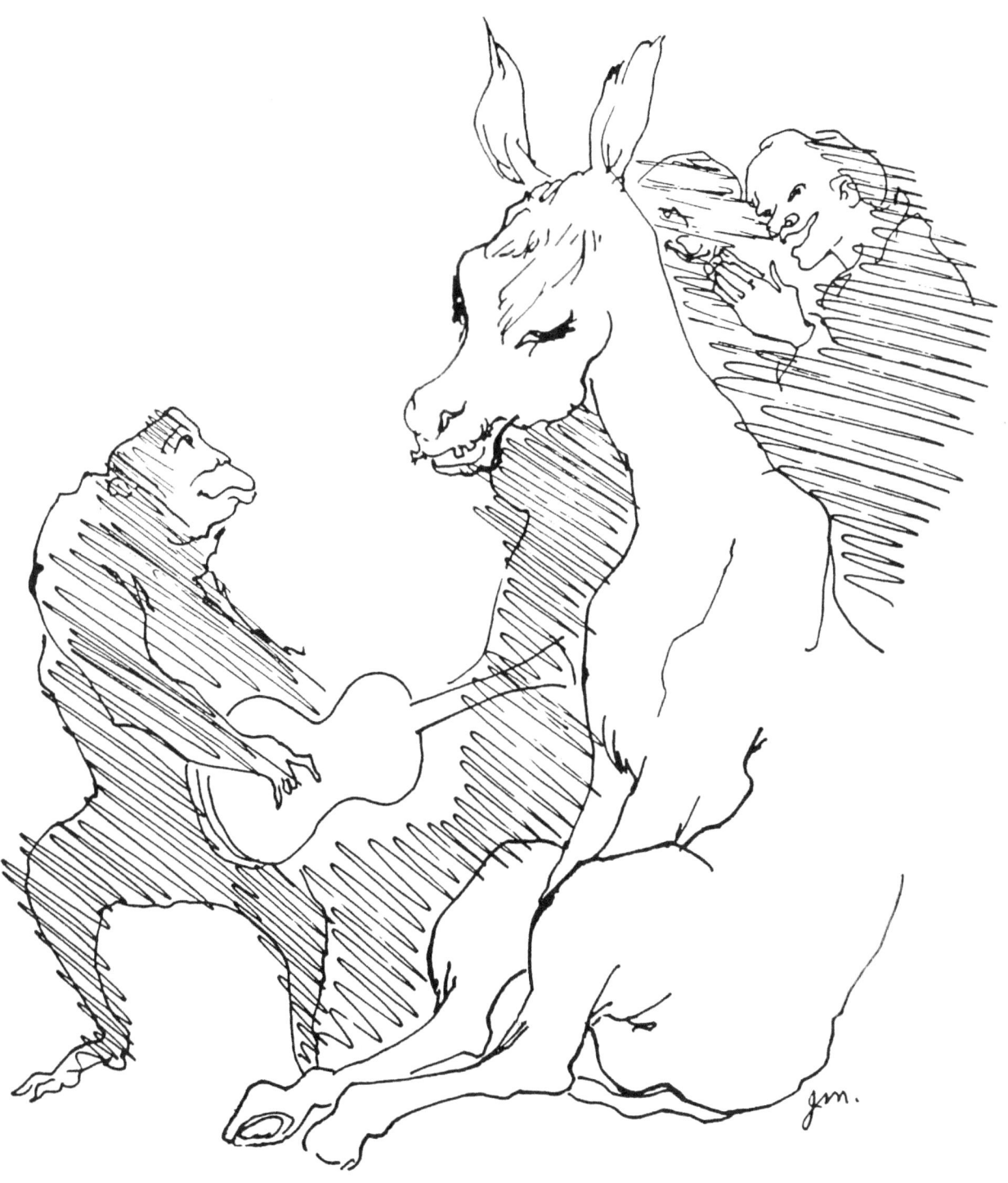

Bravo!

39. Just like his grandfather.

This poor animal has been driven mad by genealogists and coats of arms. He's not the only one.

Asta su abuelo.

A este pobre animal le han vuelto loco los genealogistas y reyes de armas. No es él solo.

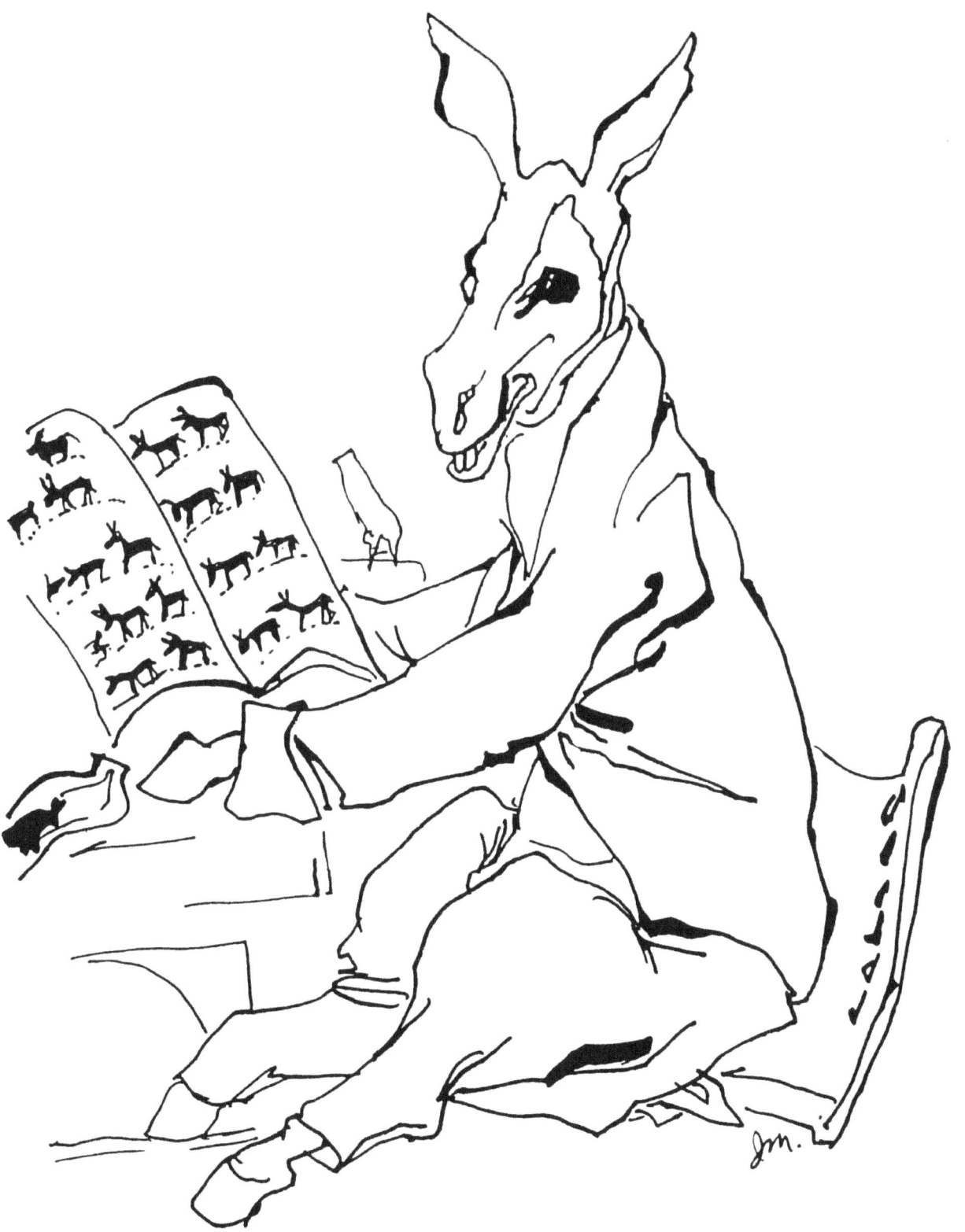

Just like his grandfather.

40. Of what evil will he die?

The doctor is excellent, thoughtful, calm, serious. What
more do you want?

De que mal morira?

El medico es excelente, meditabundo, reflexivo, pausado, serio.
¿ Que más hay que pedir?

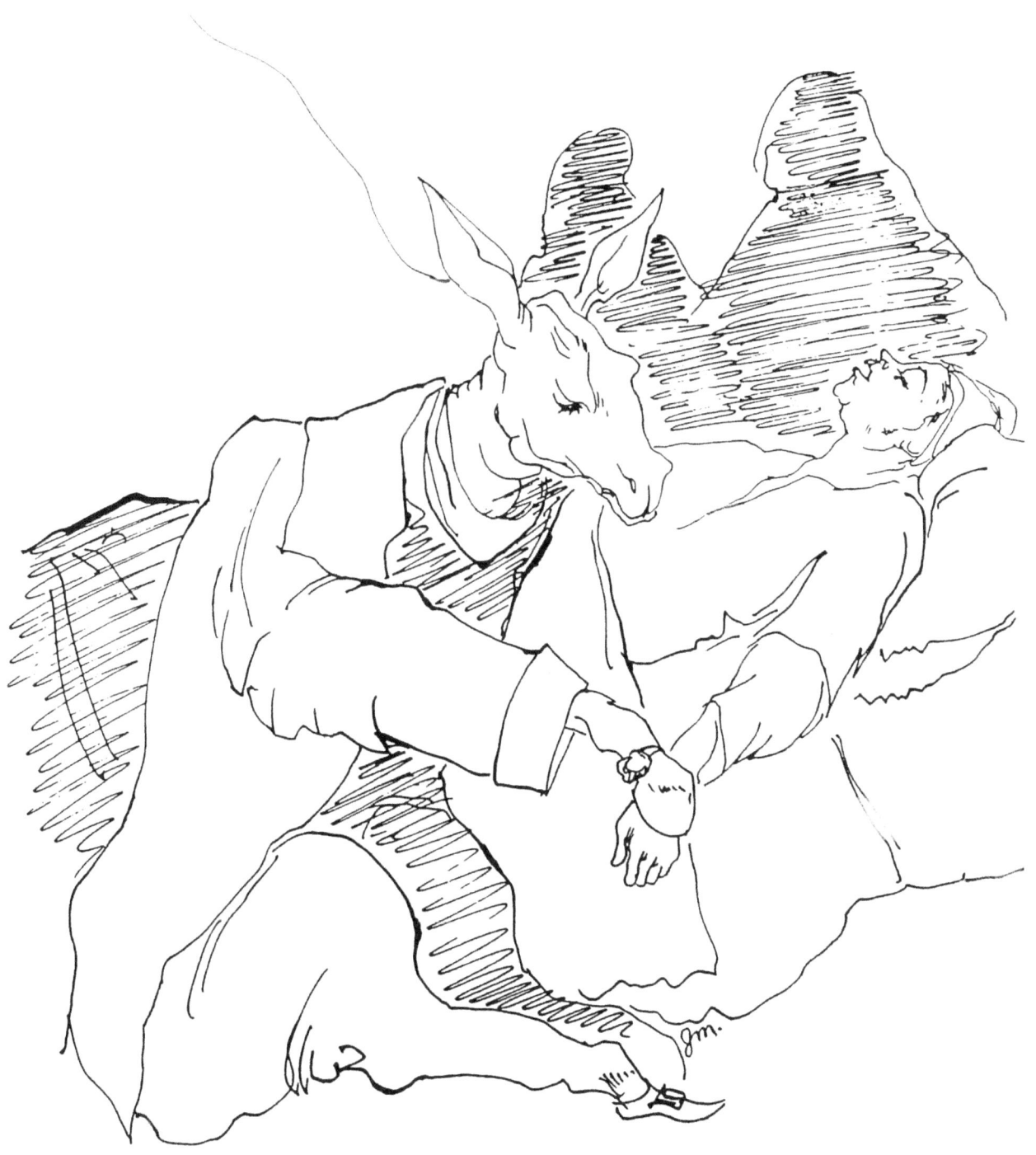

Of what evil will he die?

41. No more and no less.

Of course he should have his portrait painted. Then those who have never met him can know just who he is.

Ni mas ni menos.

Hace muy bien en retratarse; así sabrán quien es los que no le conozcan ni ayan visto.

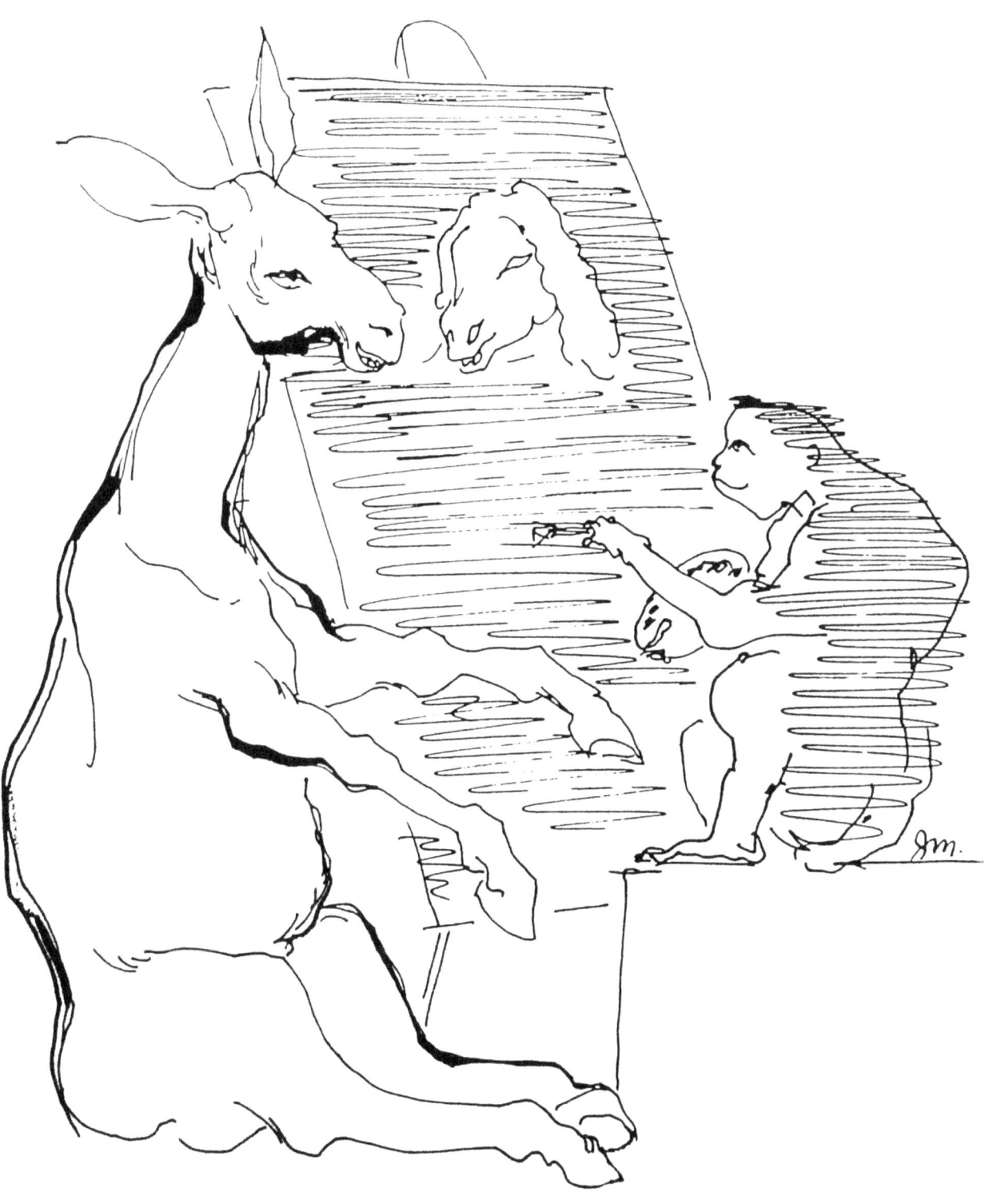

No more and no less.

42. The helpless ones.
Who would deny that these two horsemen are beasts of burden?

Tu que no puedes.
¿Quien no dirá que estos dos caballeros son caballerías?

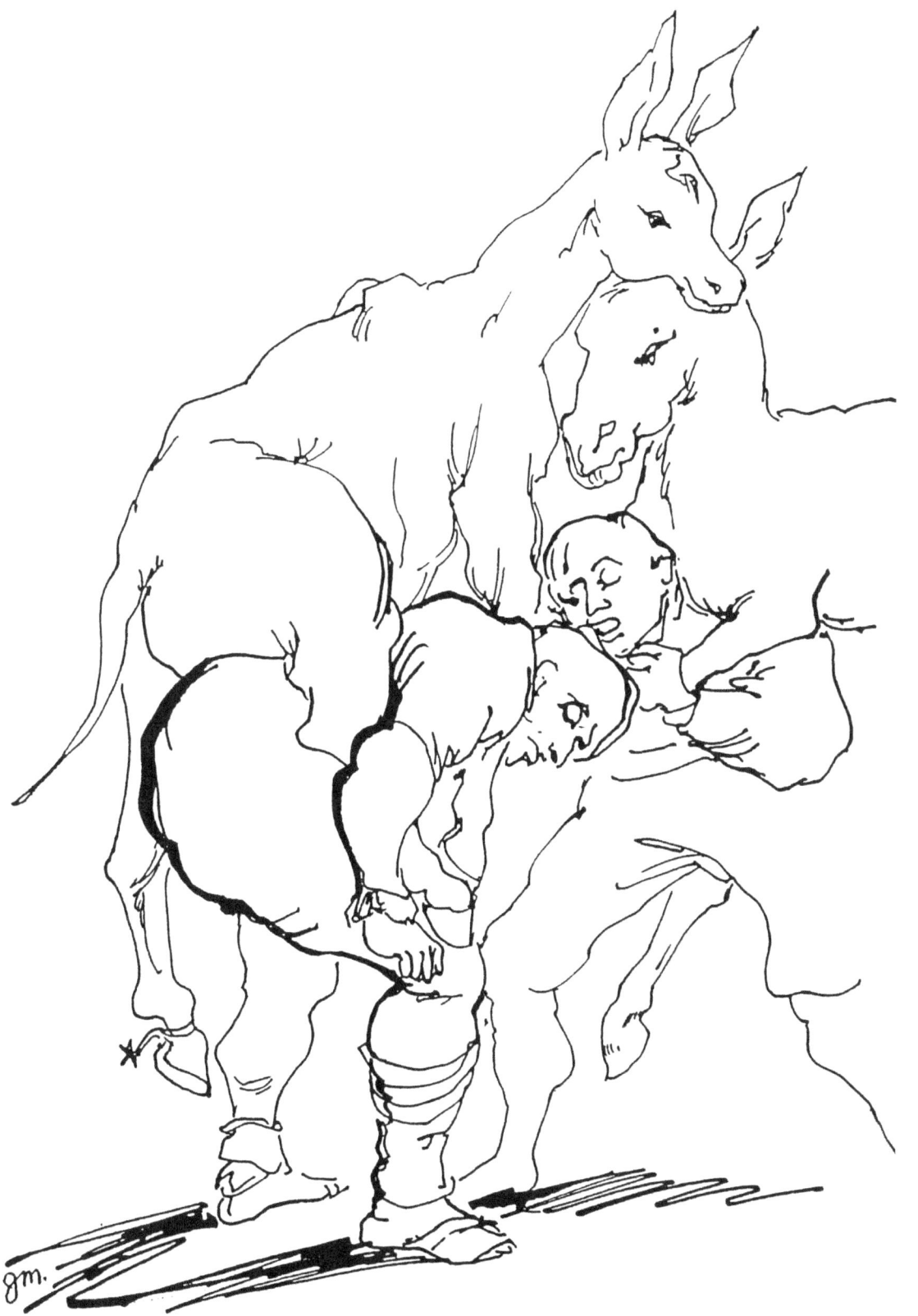

The helpless ones.

43. The sleep of reason brings forth monsters.

The sleep of reason brings forth monsters. Fantasy without reason may make monsters, but reason itself, without imagination, may create even worse demons. Imagination, deserted by reason, brings forth impossible monsters. United with reason, she is the mother of the arts and the source of their wonders.

El sueno de la razón produce monstruos.

La fantasia abandonada de la razón produce monstruos imposibles; unida con ella, es madre de las artes y origen dé sus marabillas.

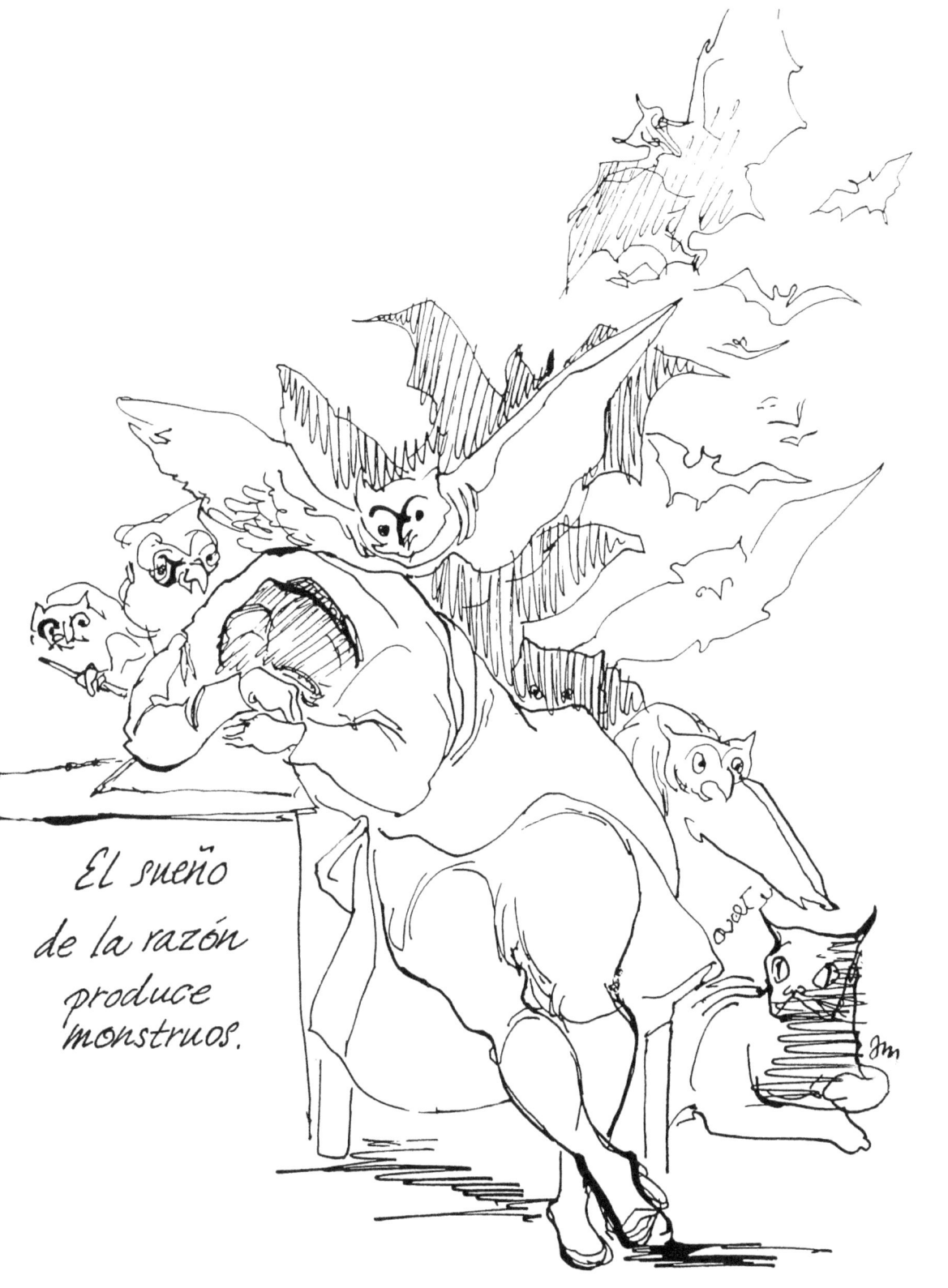

43

El sueño
de la razón
produce
monstruos.

The sleep of reason brings forth monsters.

44. Their work is fine-spun.

These witches spin so exceedingly fine that even the Devil will not be able to unravel their work.

Hilan Delgado.

Hilan delagado y la trama que urden ni el Diablo la podrá deshacer.

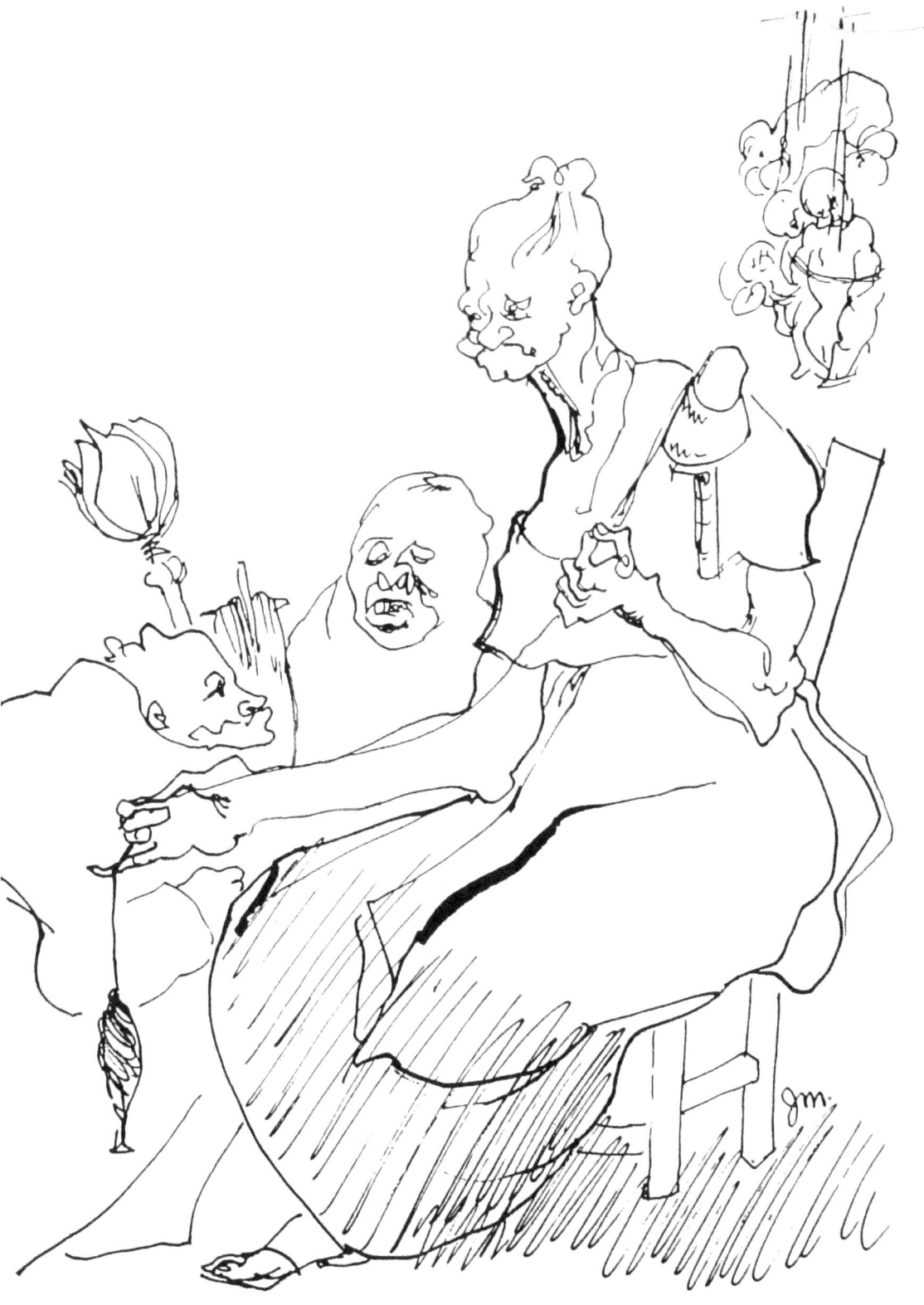

Their work is fine-spun.

45. There is a lot to suck.

The old crones suck little children; the adolescents suck grown-ups. It's as if man is born to have the very life sucked out of him for the benefit of others.

Mucho hay que chupar.

Las que llegan a 80 chupan chiquillos; las que no pasan de 18, chupan a los grandes. Parece que el hombre nace y vive para ser chupado.

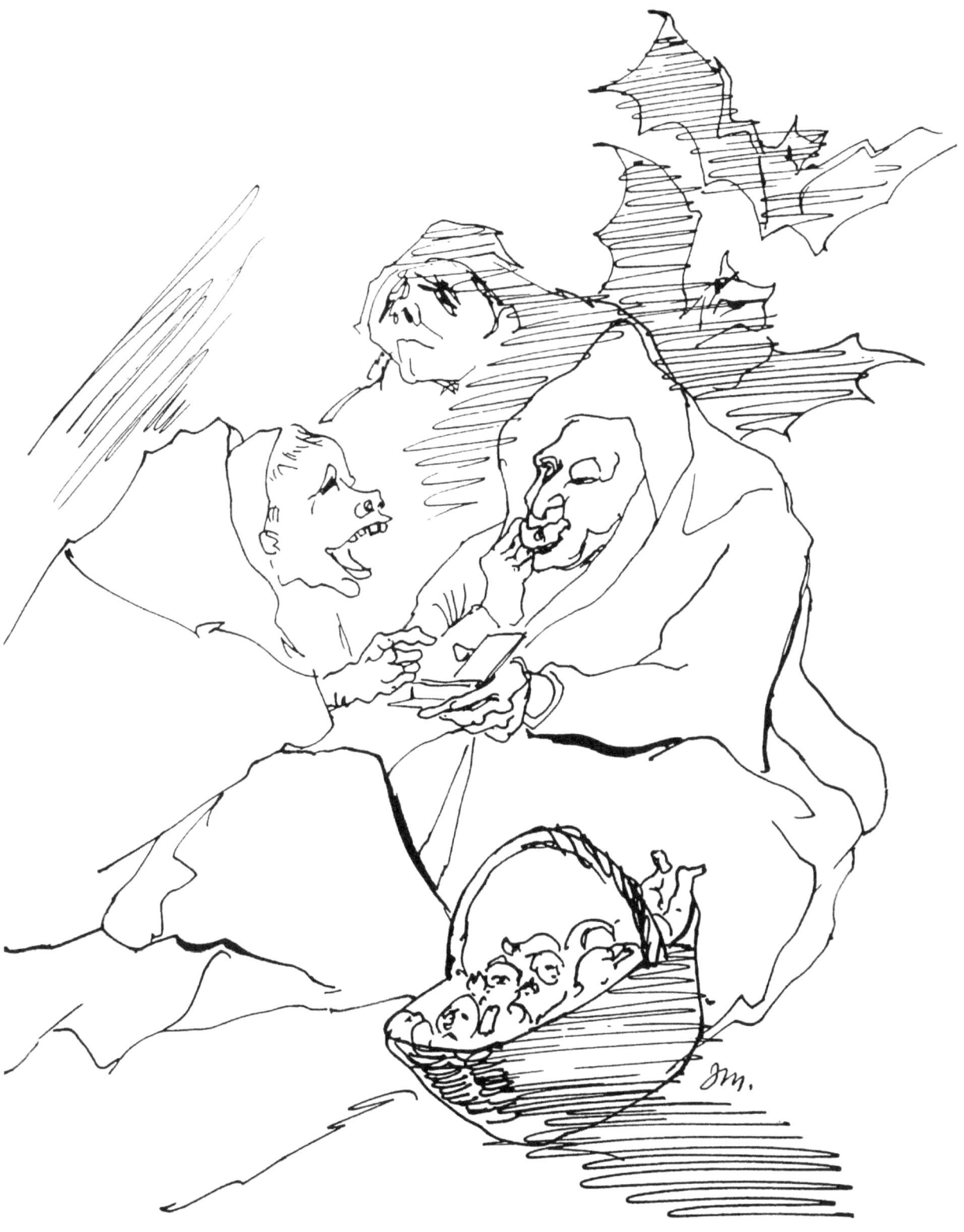

45

There is a lot to suck.

46. Correction.

In any faculty one must welcome censure and criticism but in
the School of Witchcraft one must display rare talent, dedication, enthusiasm,
docility and submission to the instruction of the supreme Witch who directs
the college at Barahona.

Corrección.

*Sin corrección ni censura no se adelanta en ninguna facultad y la de la
Brugería necesita particular talento, aplicación, edad madura, sumisión y
docilidad a los consejos del Gran Brujo que dirige el seminario de
Barahona.*

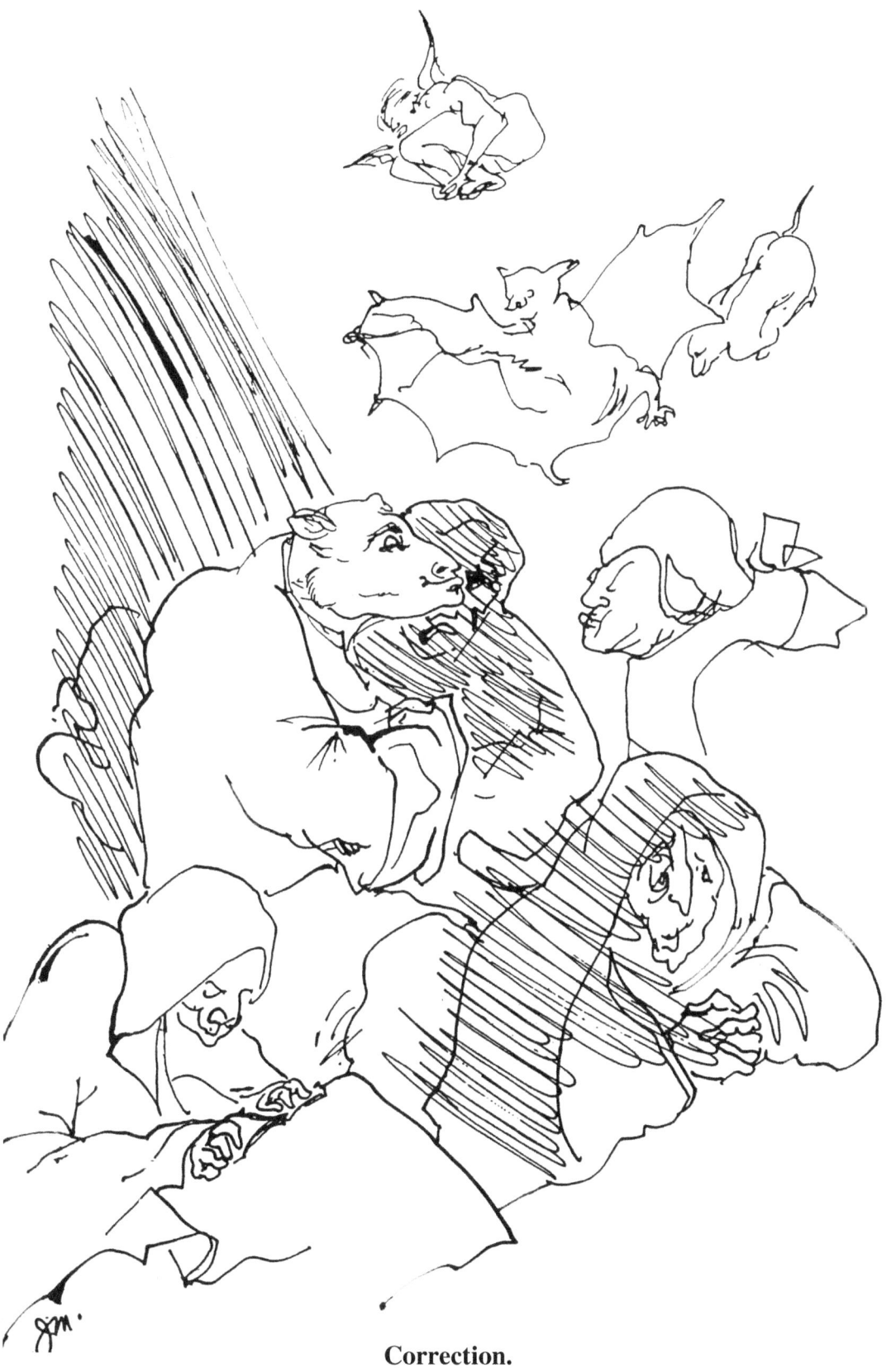

46

Correction.

47. Homage to the master.

Of course! Only ungrateful students fail to make a pilgrimage to their professor of diabolical arts who taught them everything they need to know.

Obsequio á el maestro.

Es muy justo; serían discípulos ingratos si no visitaran a su catedrático a quien deben todo lo que saben en su diabólica facultad.

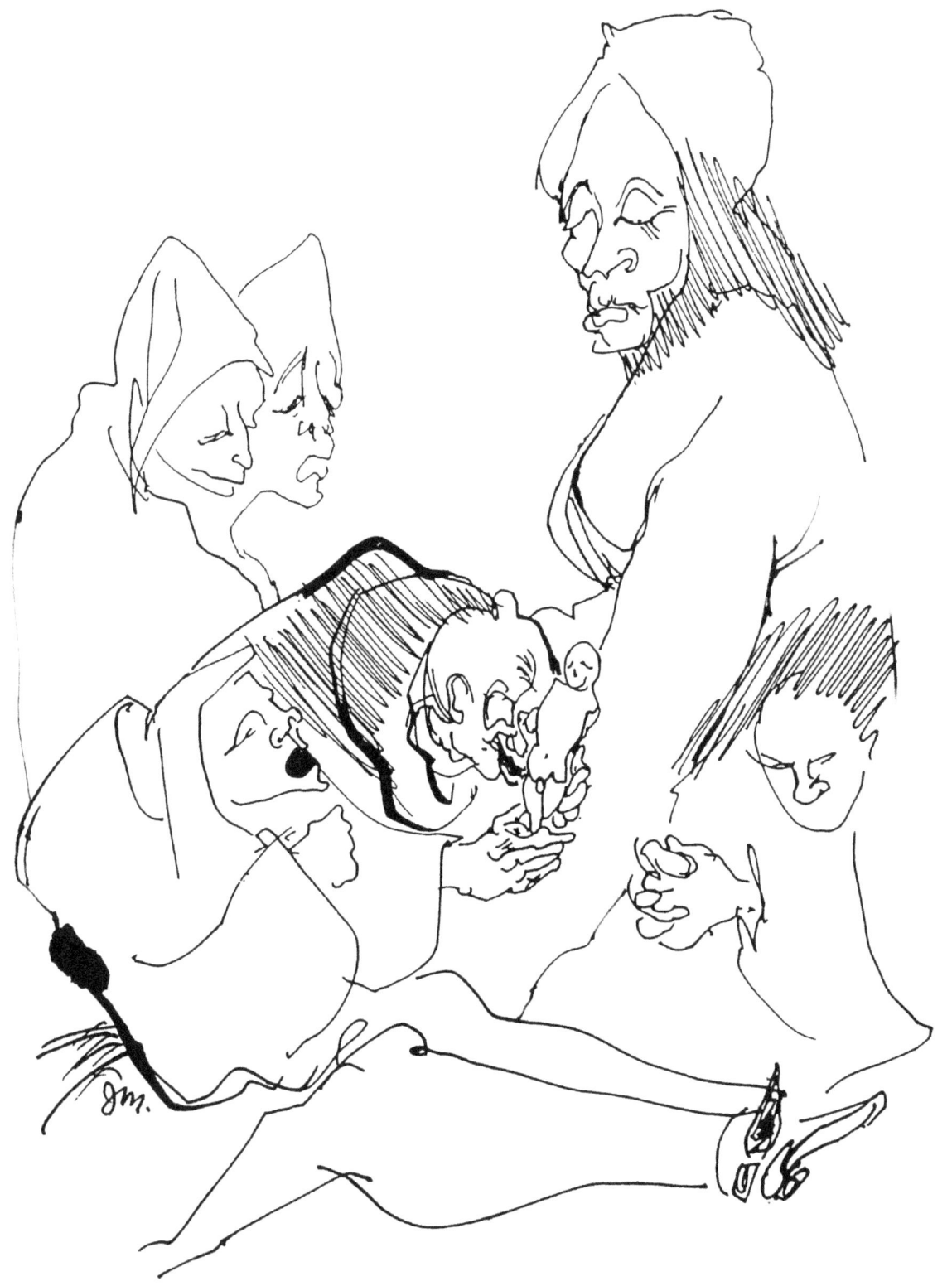

47

Homage to the master.

48. Gossips and blowhards.
The gossiping witches are the most annoying in all witchcraft and the least intelligent in the black arts. If they actually knew something important they wouldn't spread it around.

Soplones.
Los Bruxos soplones son los más fastidiosos de toda la bruxería y los menos inteligentes en aquel arte. Si supieran algo no se meterían a soplones.

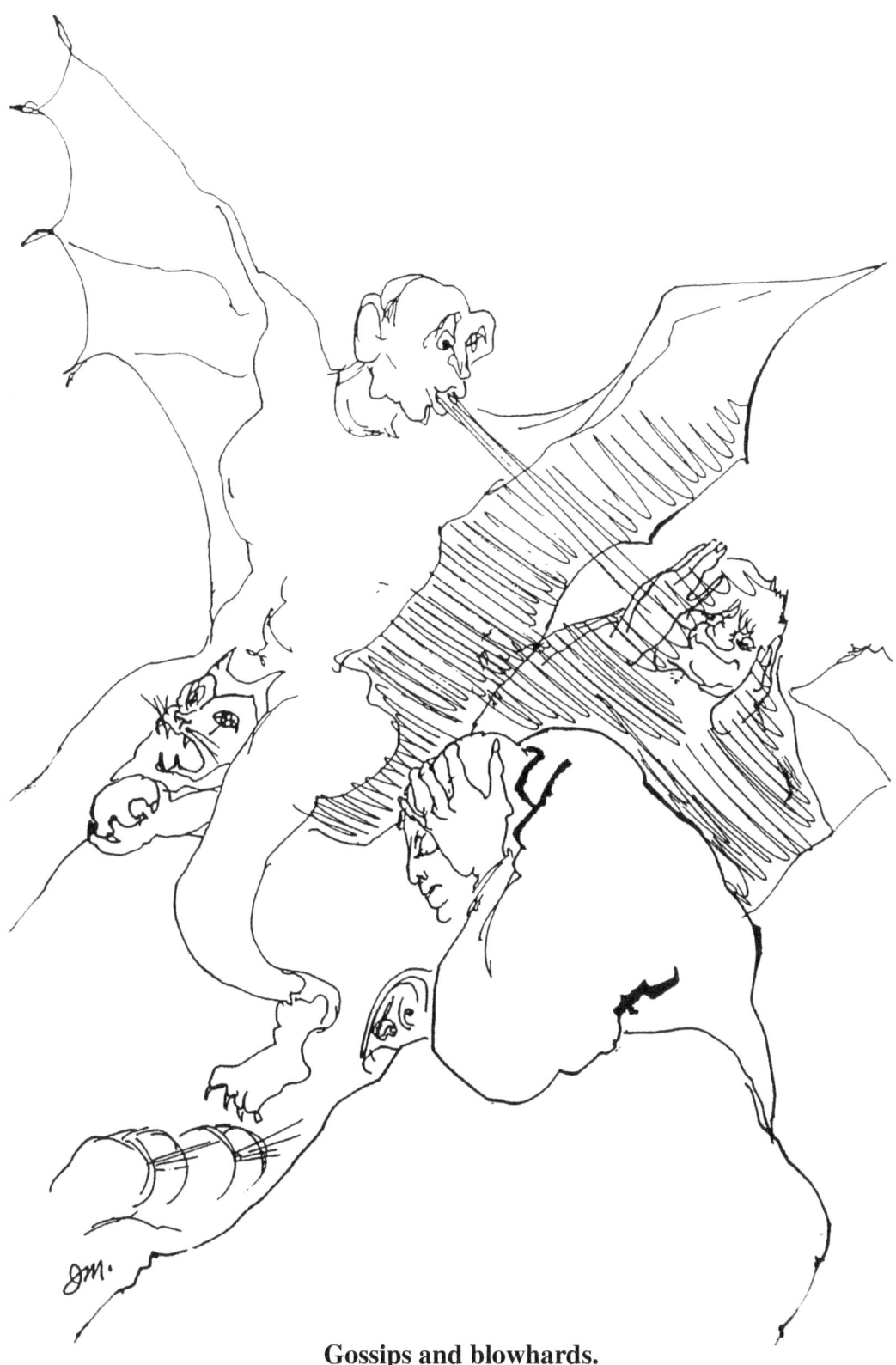

48

Gossips and blowhards.

49. Brownies.

The brownies are another kind of people. So obliging, these friendly little folks like to play practical jokes. They are very good-natured, but a little greedy.

Duendecitos.

Ésta ya es otra gente. Alegres, juguetones, serviciales; un poco golosos, amigos de pegar chascos; pero muy hombrecitos de bien.

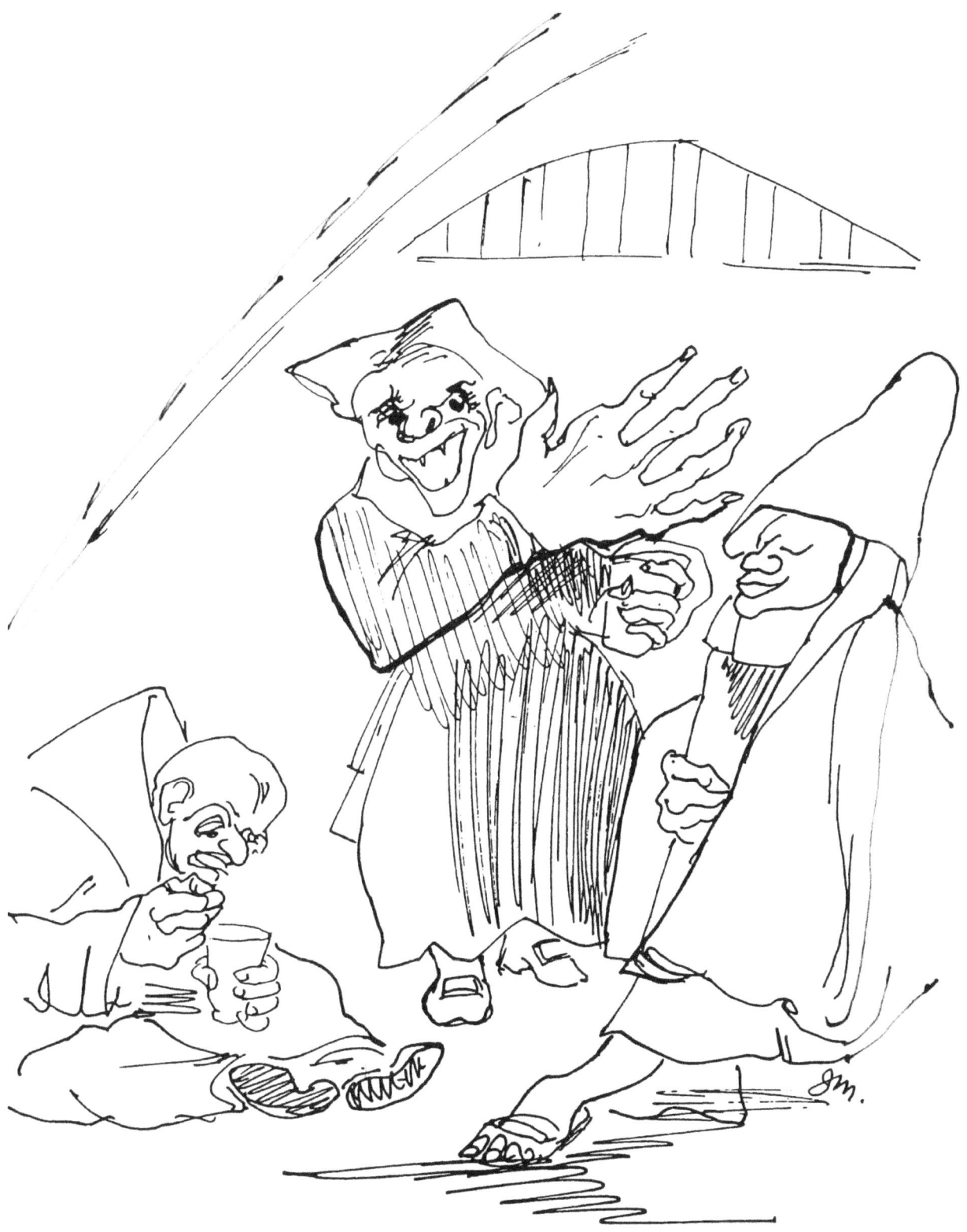

49

The brownies.

50. The passive ones.

Those who hear nothing, know nothing, do nothing, belong
to the Clan of the Passive, good for nothing. Stuff your opinions down
their gullet every evening on the TV news.

Los chinchillas.

El que no oye nada ni sabe nada, ni hace nada, pertenece a la numerosa
familia de los chinchillas que nunca a servido de nada.

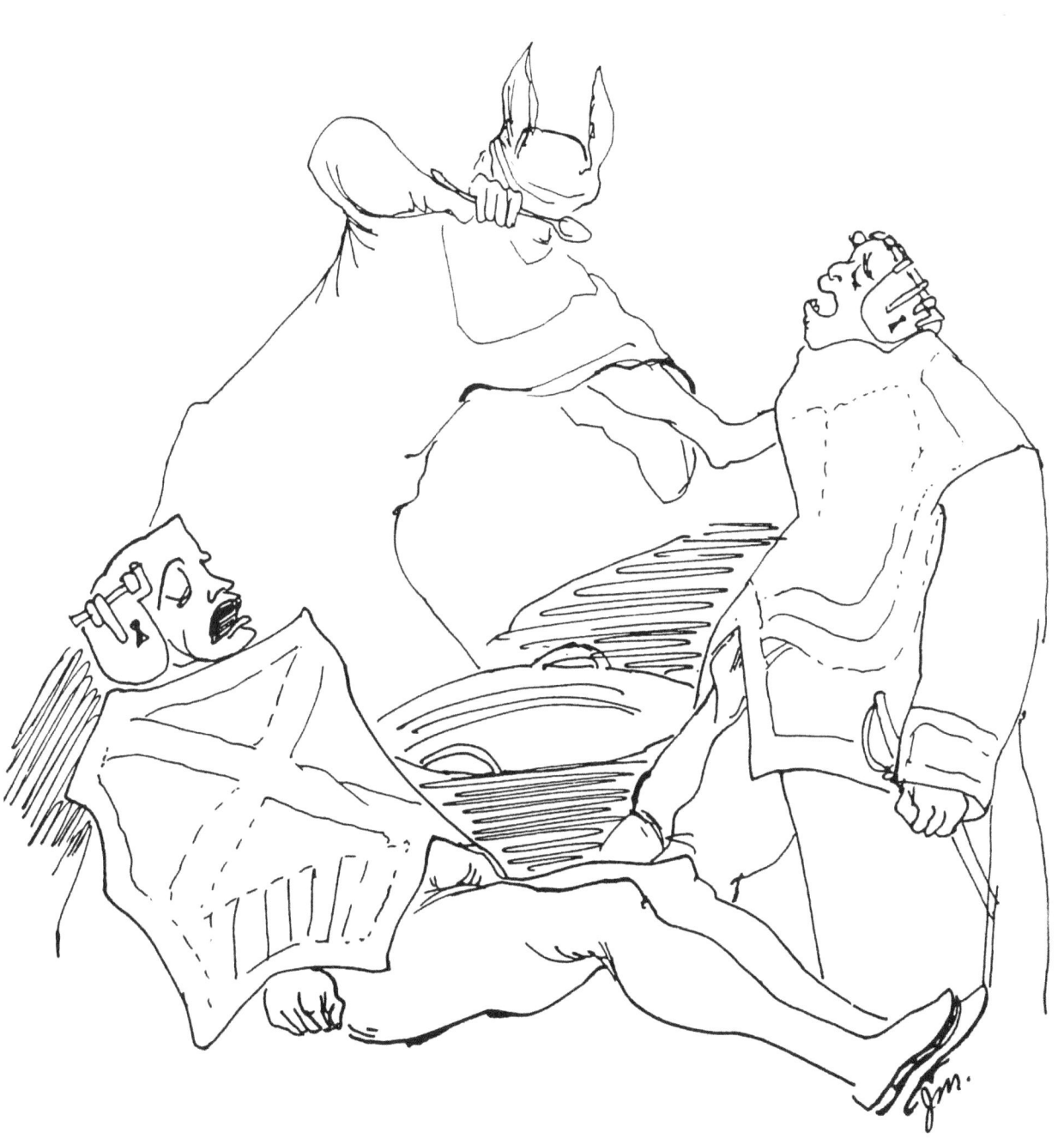

The passive ones.

51. Get a trim!

Having long nails is so disgusting that it is forbidden even in witchcraft. Get a trim!

¡Se repulen!

Esto de tener las uñas largas es tan prejudicial que aun en la bruxería está prohivido.

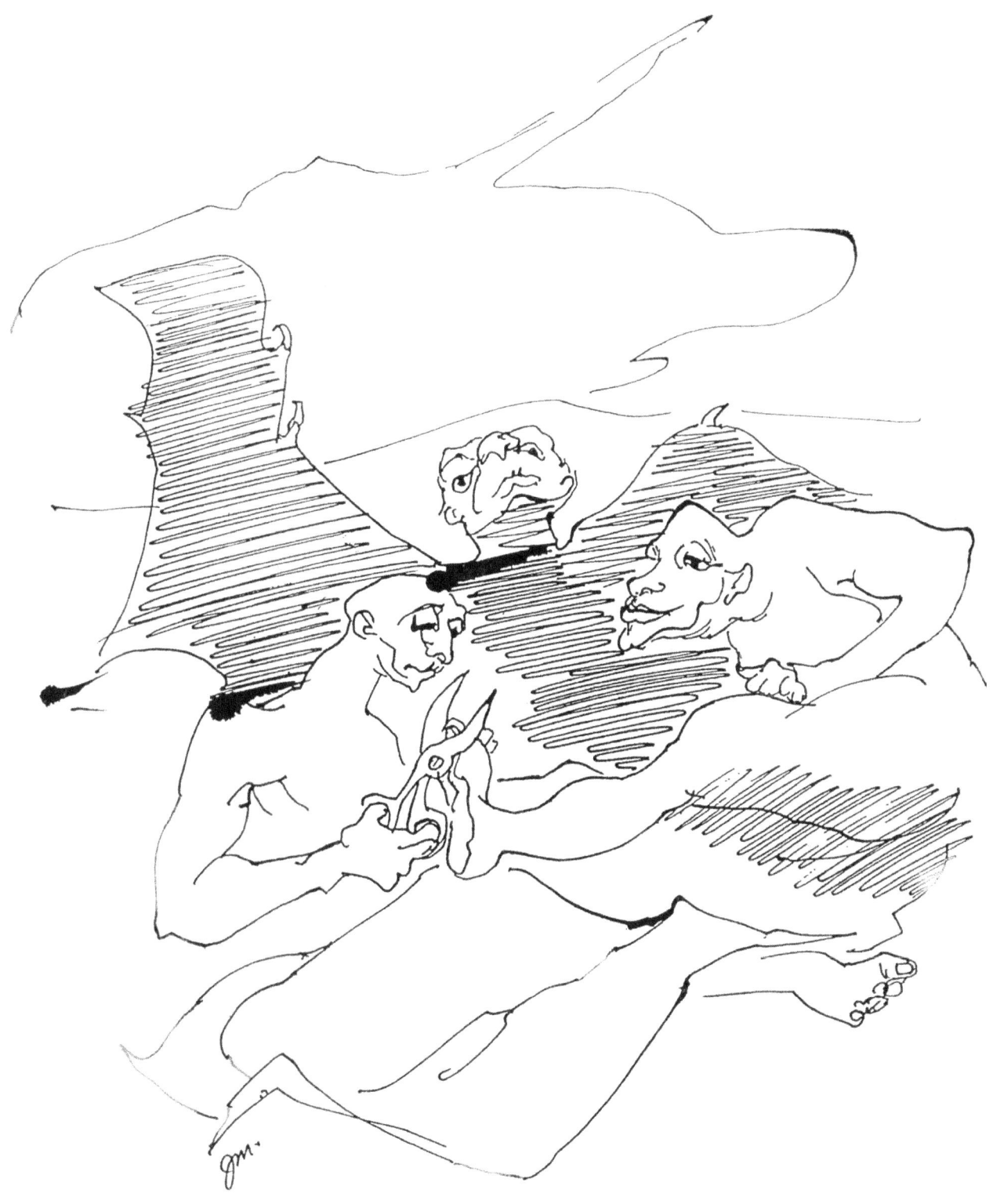

Get a trim!

52. Fine feathers make fine birds!

Many times a ridiculous nobody can be transformed into a magnificent creature.
That's what a tailor can do, with the help of those who judge things by appearances.

¡Lo que puede un sastre!

Quántas veces un bicho ridiculo se transforma de repente en un fantasmón que no es nada y aparenta mucho. Tanto puede la hablilidad de un sastre y la bobería de quien juzga las cosas por lo que parecen.

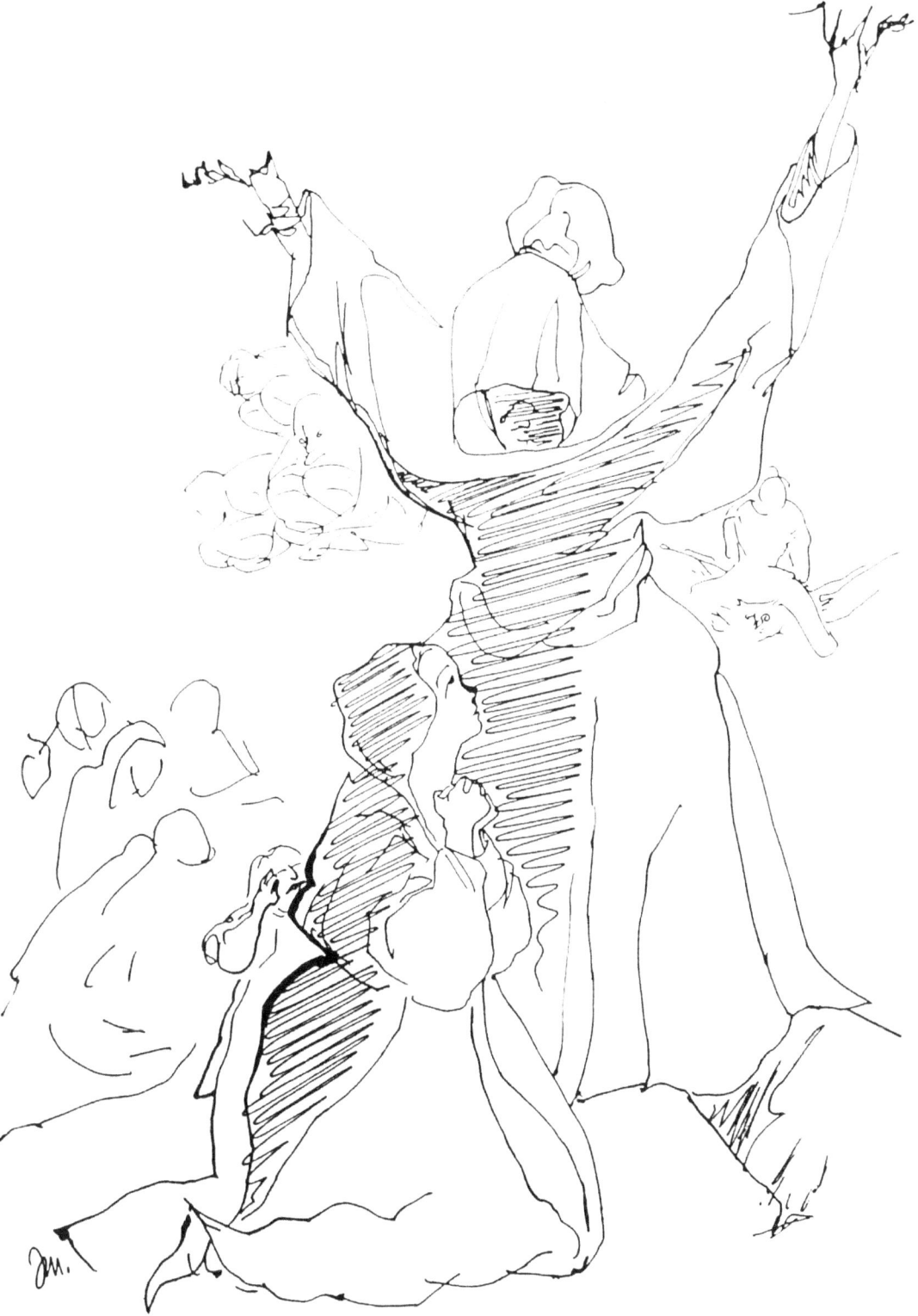

Fine feathers make fine birds!

53. What a silver tongue!

This looks like a faculty meeting. Is the parrot speaking
about medicine? Don't believe a word he says! Many a doctor
has a silver tongue but when it comes to prescriptions he just
writes at random. He babbles about pain but can't cure it. He
makes fools of the sick and fills the cemetery with skulls.

¡Que pico de oro!

*Esto tiene trazas de junta académica. ¿Quién sabe si el papagayo estará
hablando de medicina? Pero no hay que creerlo sobre su palabra.
Médico hay que quando habla es un pico do oro y quando receta un
Erodes; discurre perfectamente de las dolencias y no las cura; enboba a
los enfermos y atesta los cementerios de calaberas.*

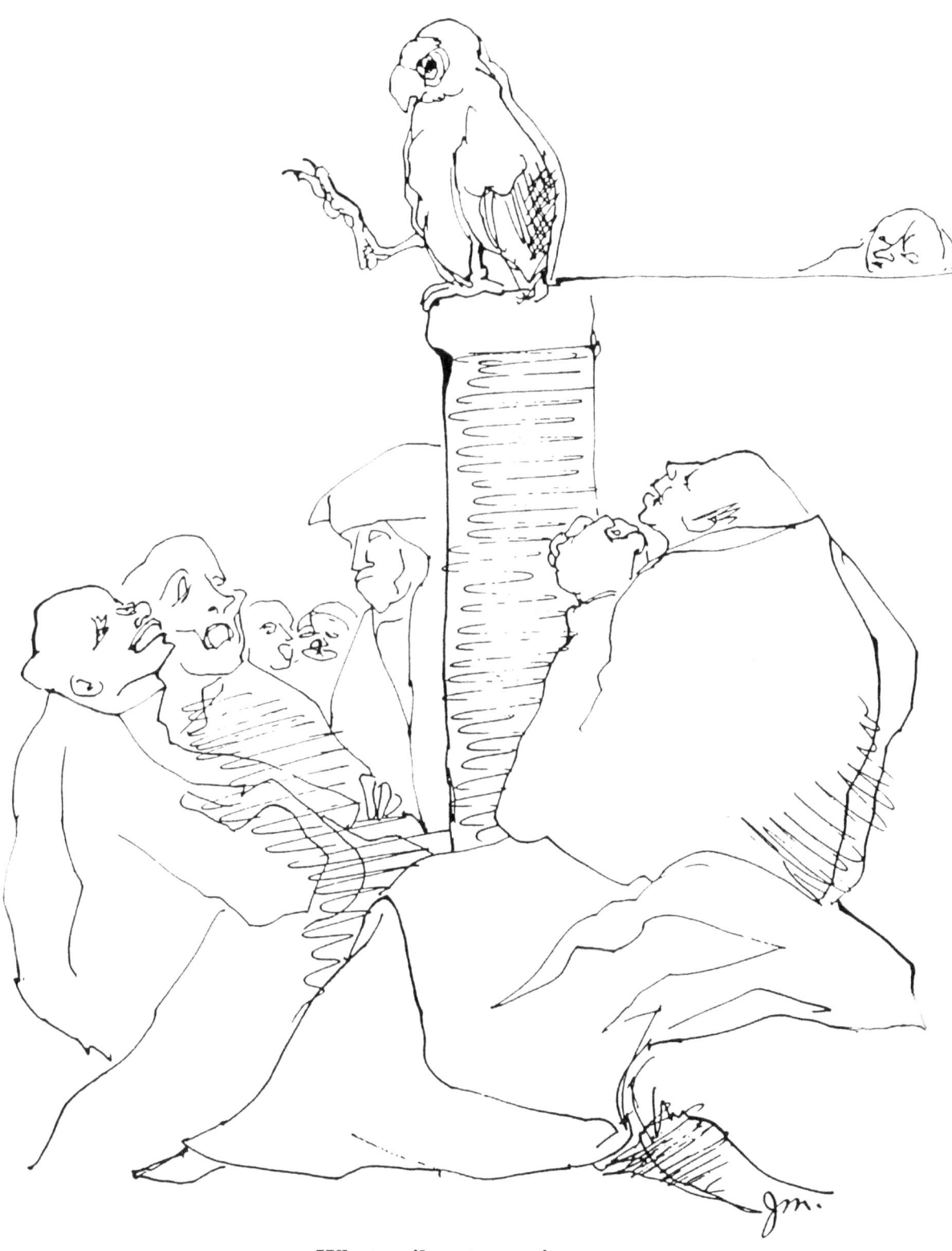

53

What a silver tongue!

54. The one who is shamefaced.

Some men have faces that are so unfortunate and indecent that they should be hidden inside their pants.

El Vergonzoso.

Hay hombres cuya cara es lomas indecent de todo su cuerpo y seria bien que los que las tienen tan desgraciada y ridicula se la metieran en los calzones.

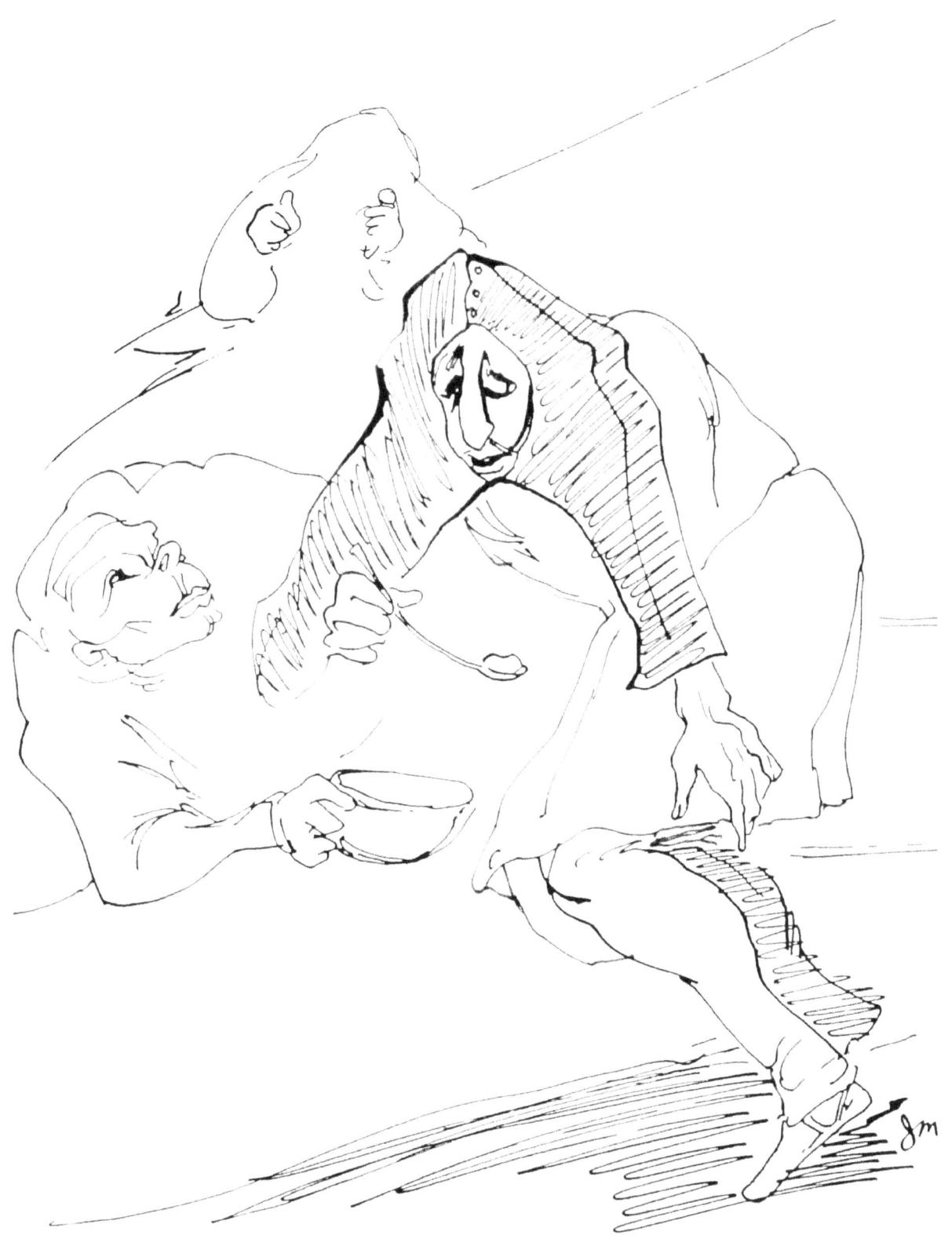

The one who is shamefaced.

55. Hurry up, death.

Of course she must doll herself up. Her little girlfriends are coming to see her because it is her 75th birthday.

Hasta la muerte.

Hace muy bien de ponerse guapa. Son sus días; cumple 75 años, y bendrán las amigitas a verla.

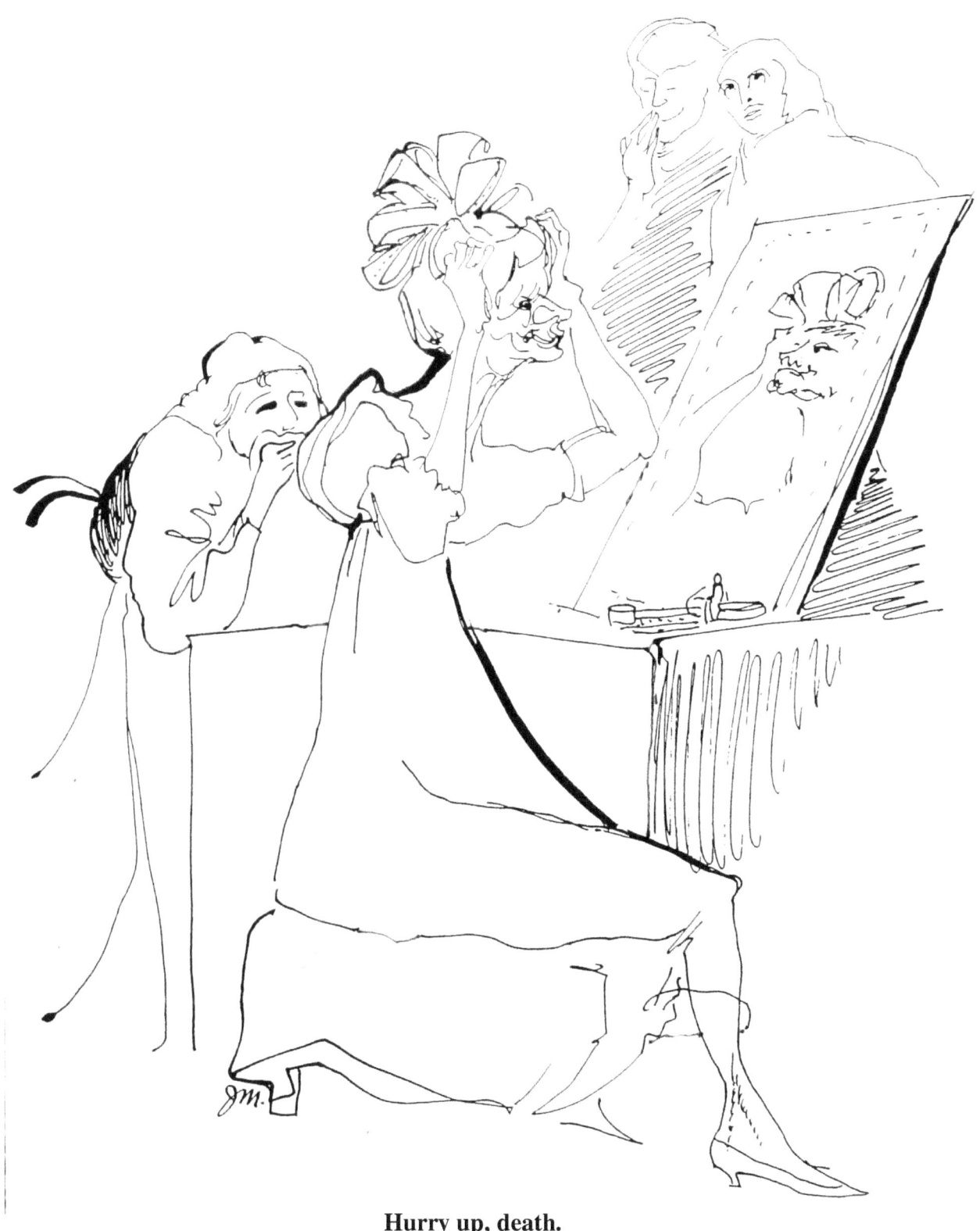

Hurry up, death.

56. Rising and falling.

Fickle fortune mistreats everyone who courts her. Efforts to rise are
rewarded with hot air and she punishes those who have risen by bringing
their downfall.

Subir y bajar.

La fortuna trata muy mal a quien la osequia. Paga con humo
la fatiga de subir y al que ha subido le castiga con precipitarle.

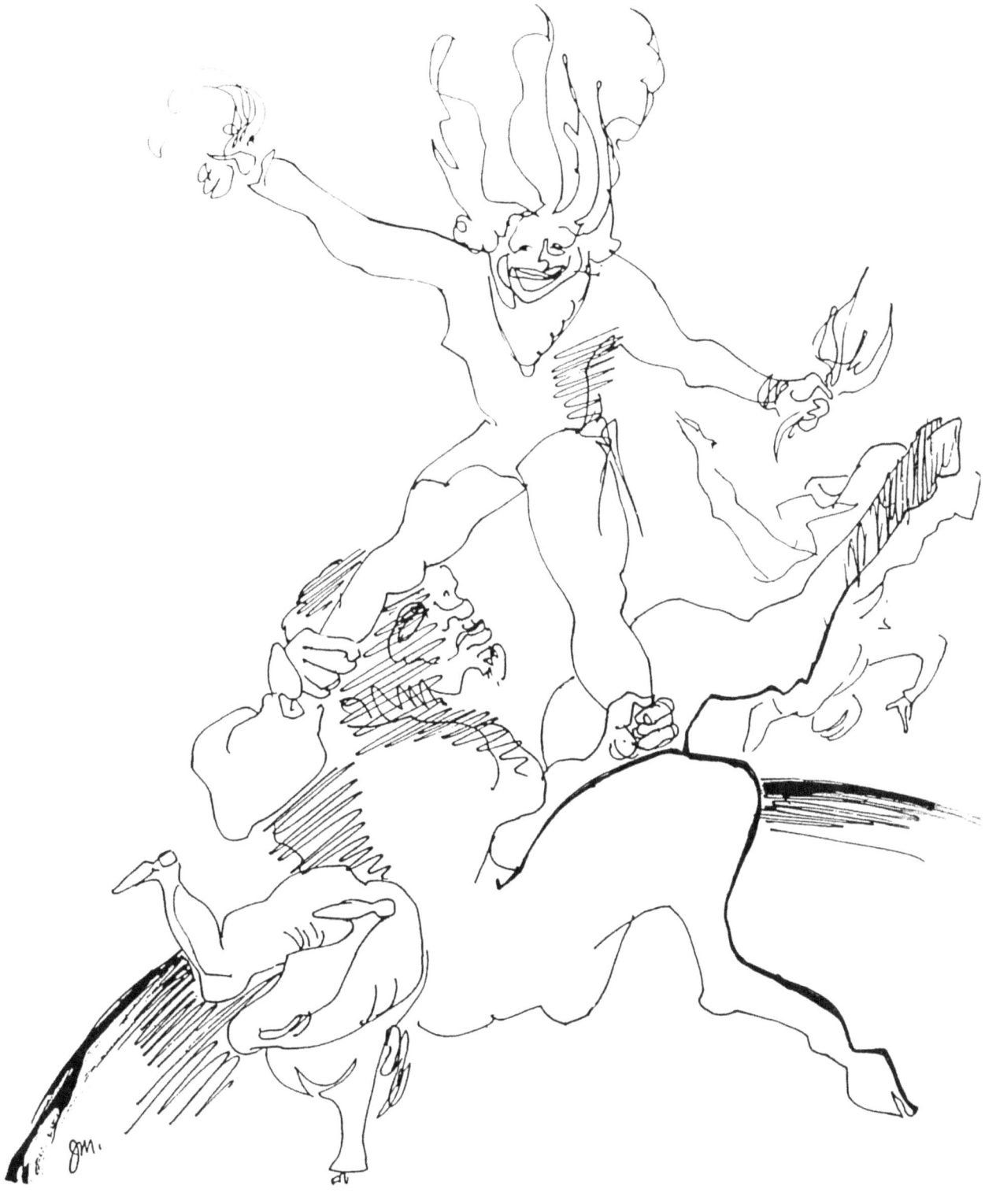

Rising and falling.

56

57. The family tree.

The fiancée is fooled by letting him see her pedigree: her parents,
grandparents, great grandparents, and great, great grandparents.
But who is she? He'll find out soon enough.

La filiacion.

*Aquí se trata de engatusar al novio haciendole ver por la egecutoria
quienes fueron los padres, abuelos, visabuelos y tatarabuelos de la
señorita; y ella, ¿quien es? Luego la verá.*

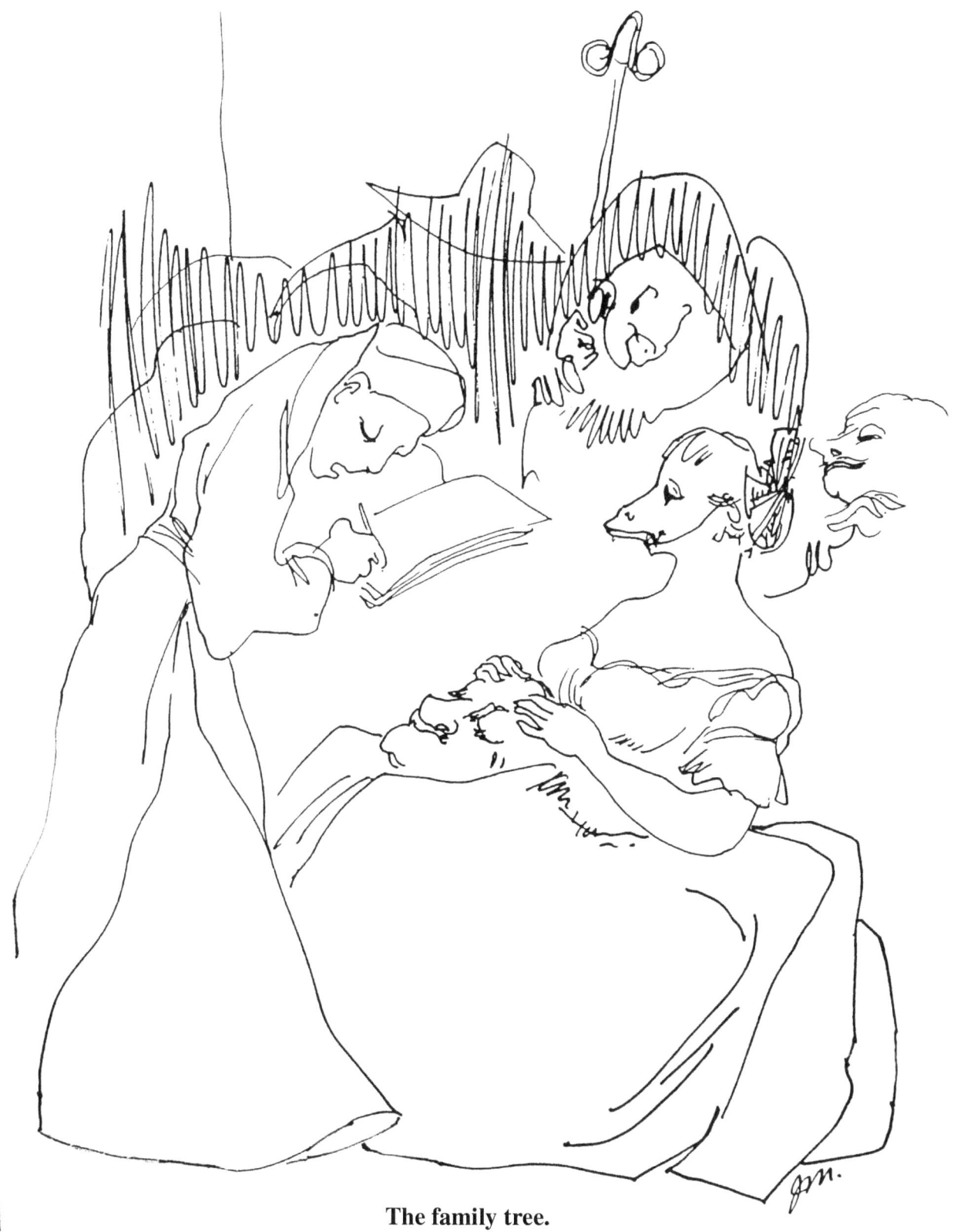

57

The family tree.

58. Take that, you dog!

If you live among people you will learn to loathe it. If you want to avoid that you must go and live alone in the mountains. But when you are there you'll discover that living alone is also loathsome.

Tragala perro!

El que viva entre los hombres será geringado irremediablemente; si quiere evitarlo, habrá de irse a habitar los montes y quando esté allí conocerá también que esto de vivir solo es una geringa.

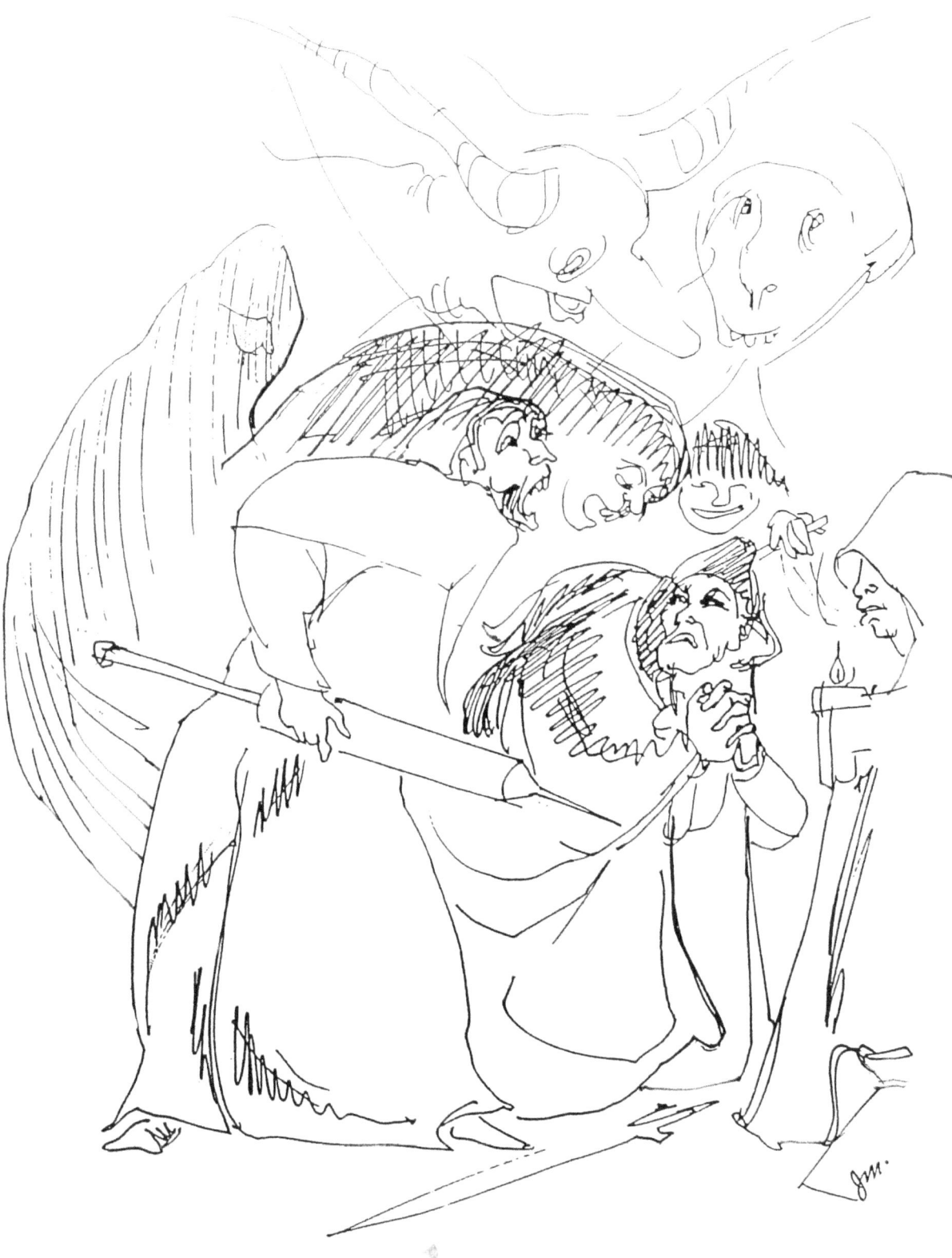

58

Take that, you dog!

59. Still, they're not leaving!

He who doesn't know that fortune is fickle sleeps peacefully
surrounded by dangers. He has no idea how to avoid the danger
around him and he's surprised by every misfortune.

Y aun no se van!

*El que no reflexiona sobre la instabilidad de la fortuna duerme tranquilo
rodeado de peligros; ni sabe evitar el daño que hamenaza ni hay desgracia
que no le sorprenda.*

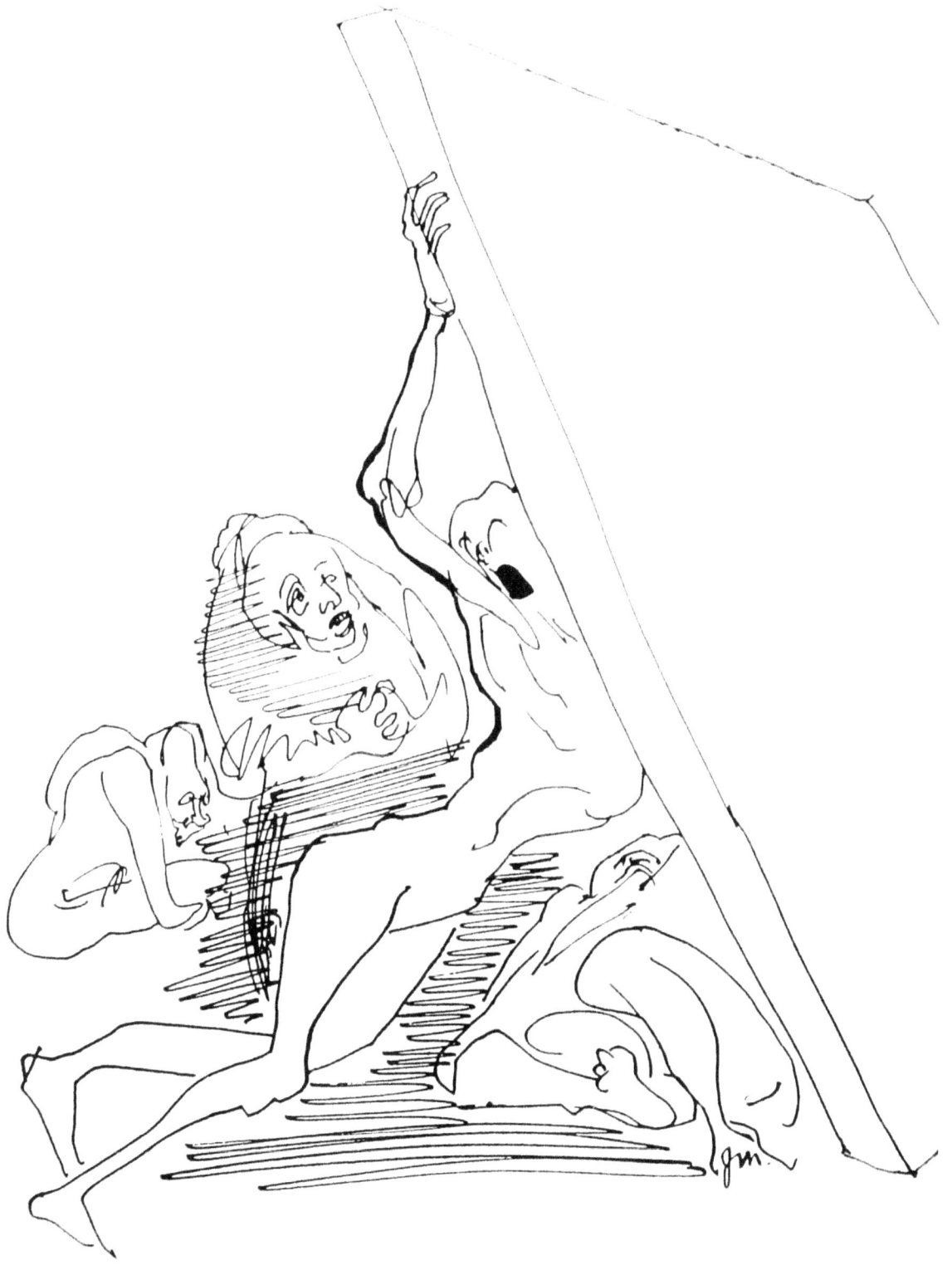

Still, they're not leaving!

60. Tests.

Little by little she is learning her lessons. Already she is taking her first steps and in time she'll be as skilled as her teacher.

Ensayos.

Poco a poco se va adelantando, ya hace pinitos y con el tiempo sabrá tanto como su maestra.

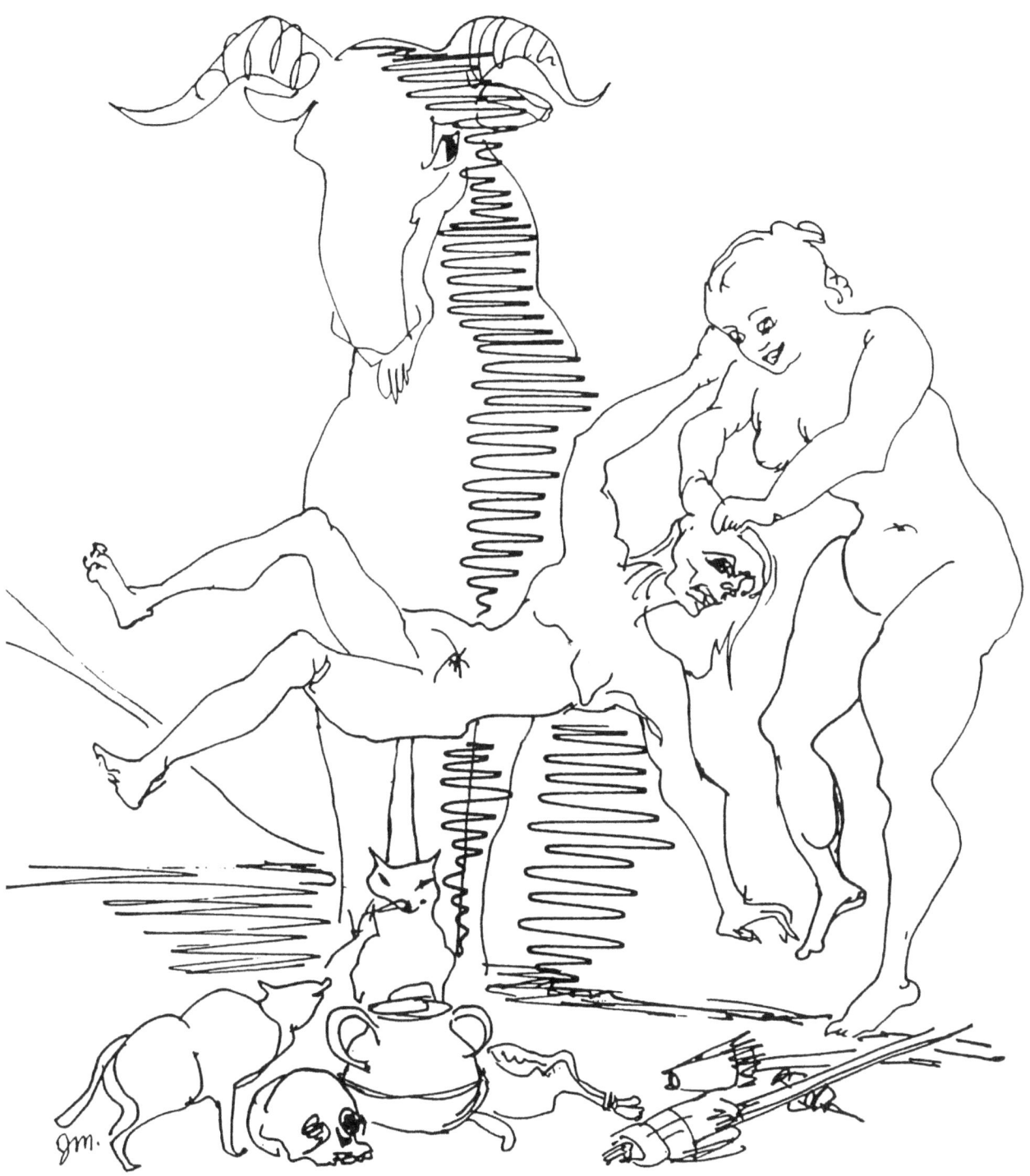

Tests.

61. They've all flown.

The three witches supporting this fashionable lady are not
really needed; they are only there as ornaments. There are
heads so full of inflammable gas that they need no balloons
or witches to make them fly.

Volaverunt.

*El grupo debrujas que sirbe de peana a la petrimetra más que necesidad
es adorno. Hay cabezas tan llenas de gas inflammable que no necesitan
para volvar ni globo ni brujas.*

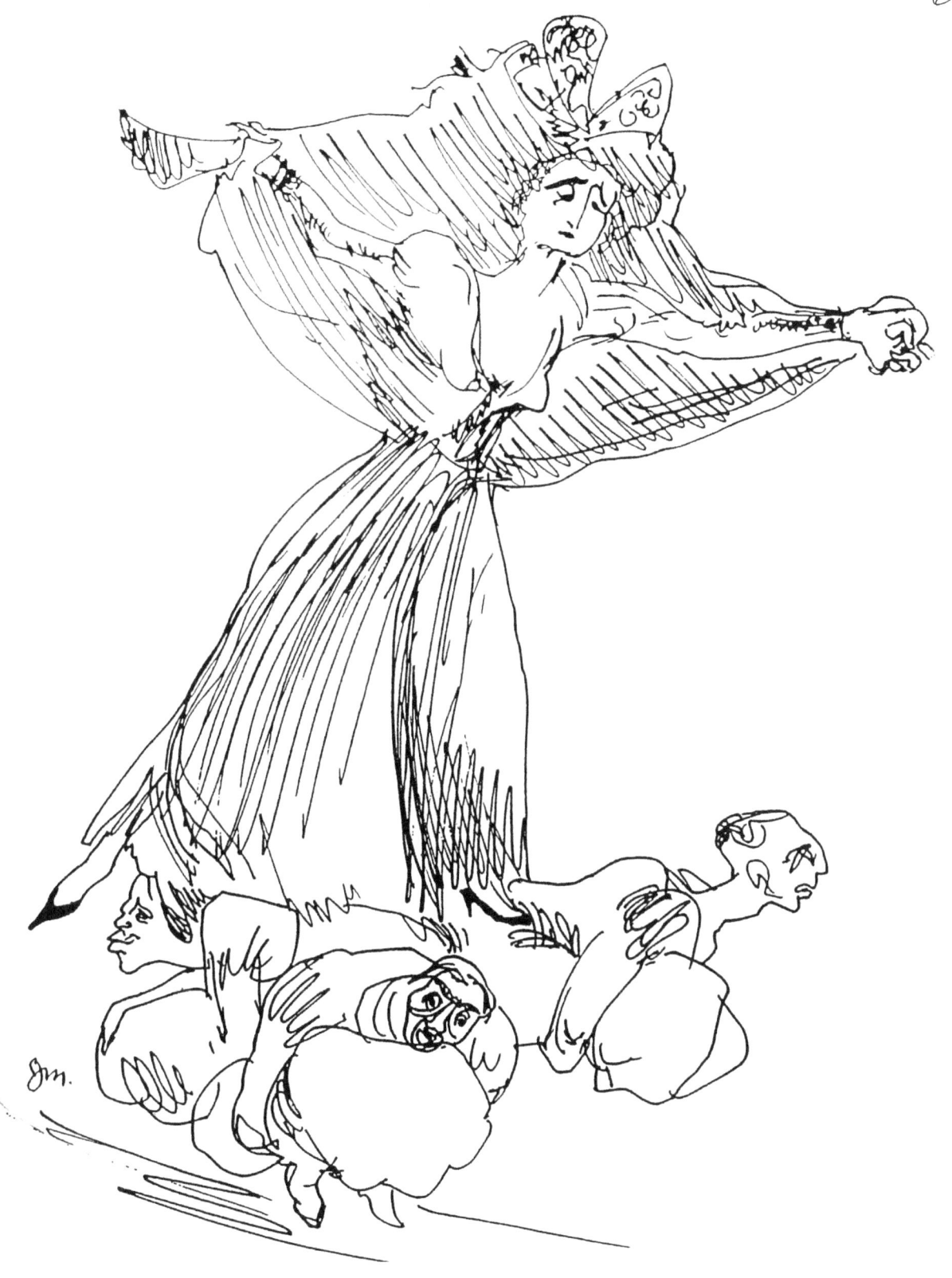

61

They've all flown.

62. Who would have thought it!

This terrible quarrel is about which of them is the greatest witch. Who would have thought the screechy one and the grizzly one would tear each other's hair out like this? But they are accomplices, not friends. Friendship, is the daughter of virtue and these two are great villains.

¡Quien lo creyera!

Ve aquí una pelotera cruel sobre quál es más bruja de las dos. ¿Quién diria que la petiñosa y la crespa se repelaran así? La amistad es hija de la virtud: Los malbados pueden ser cómplices, pero amigos no.

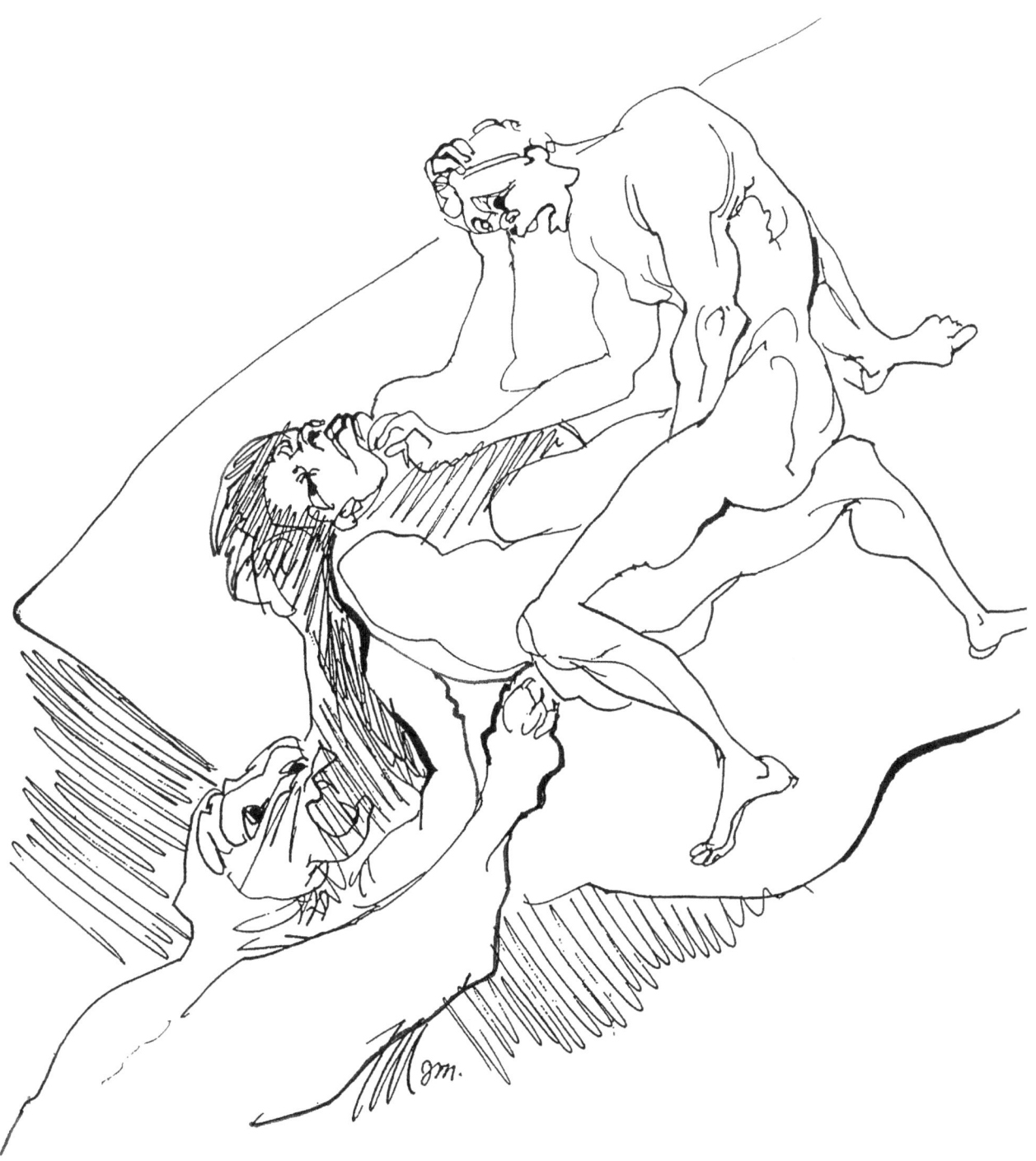

62

Who would have thought it!

63. Look how serious they are!

Here's a print showing two rich and famous witches going out for a little exercise on horseback.

¡Miren que grabes!

La estampa indica que éstos son dos brujos de conbeniencias y autoridad que han salido a hacer un poco de exercicio a caballo.

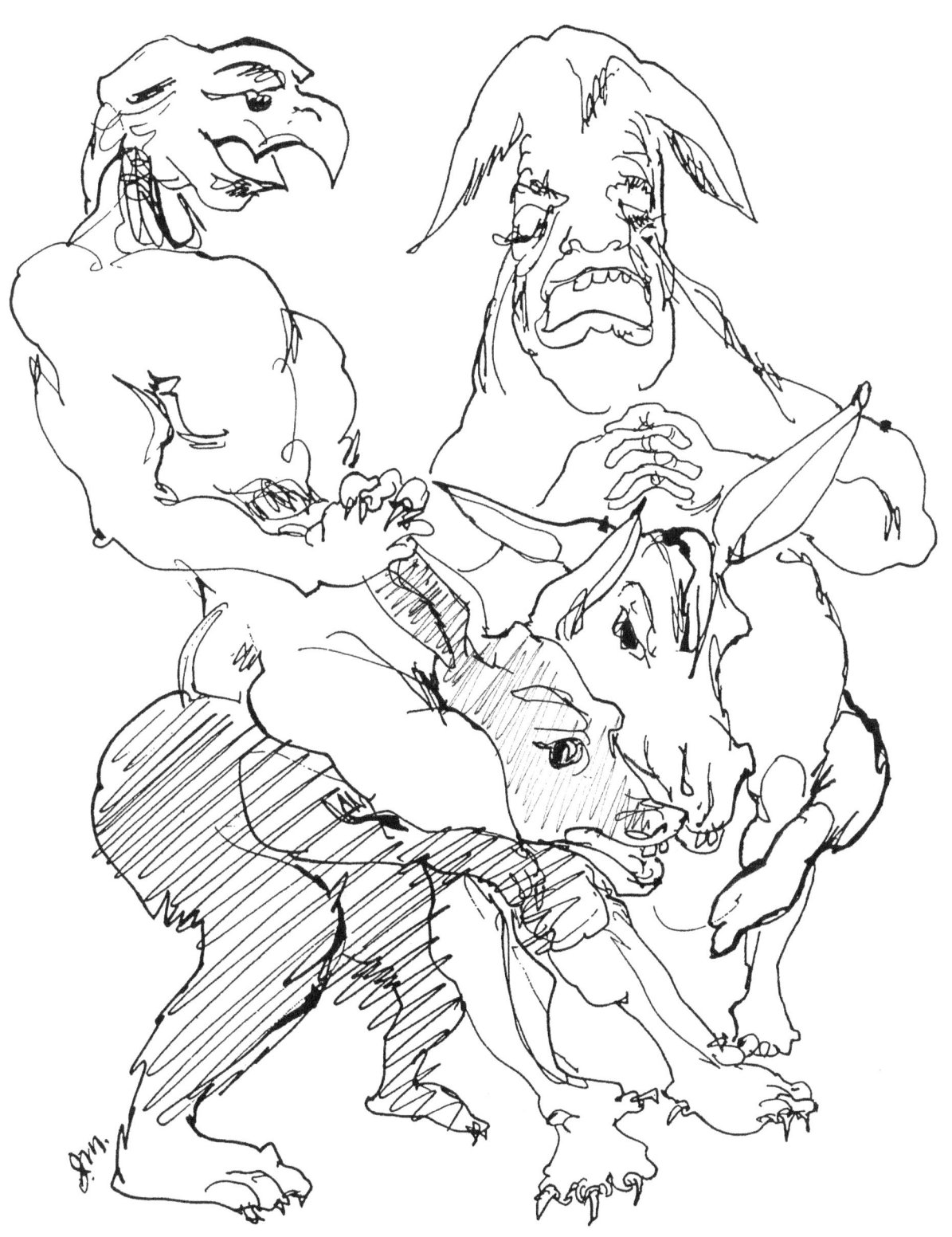

63

Look how serious they are!

64. Bon Voyage!

In the darkness this diabolical company is invisible. If it were broad daylight the whole crowd would get shot down. Where are they off to, filling the night with their infernal racket?

¡Buen Viaje!

A donde irá esta caterba infernal, dando aullidos por el aire, entre las tinieblas de la noche. Aun si fuera de dia ya era otra cosa y a fuerza de escopetazos caería al suelo toda la gorullada, pero como es de noche, nadie las ve.

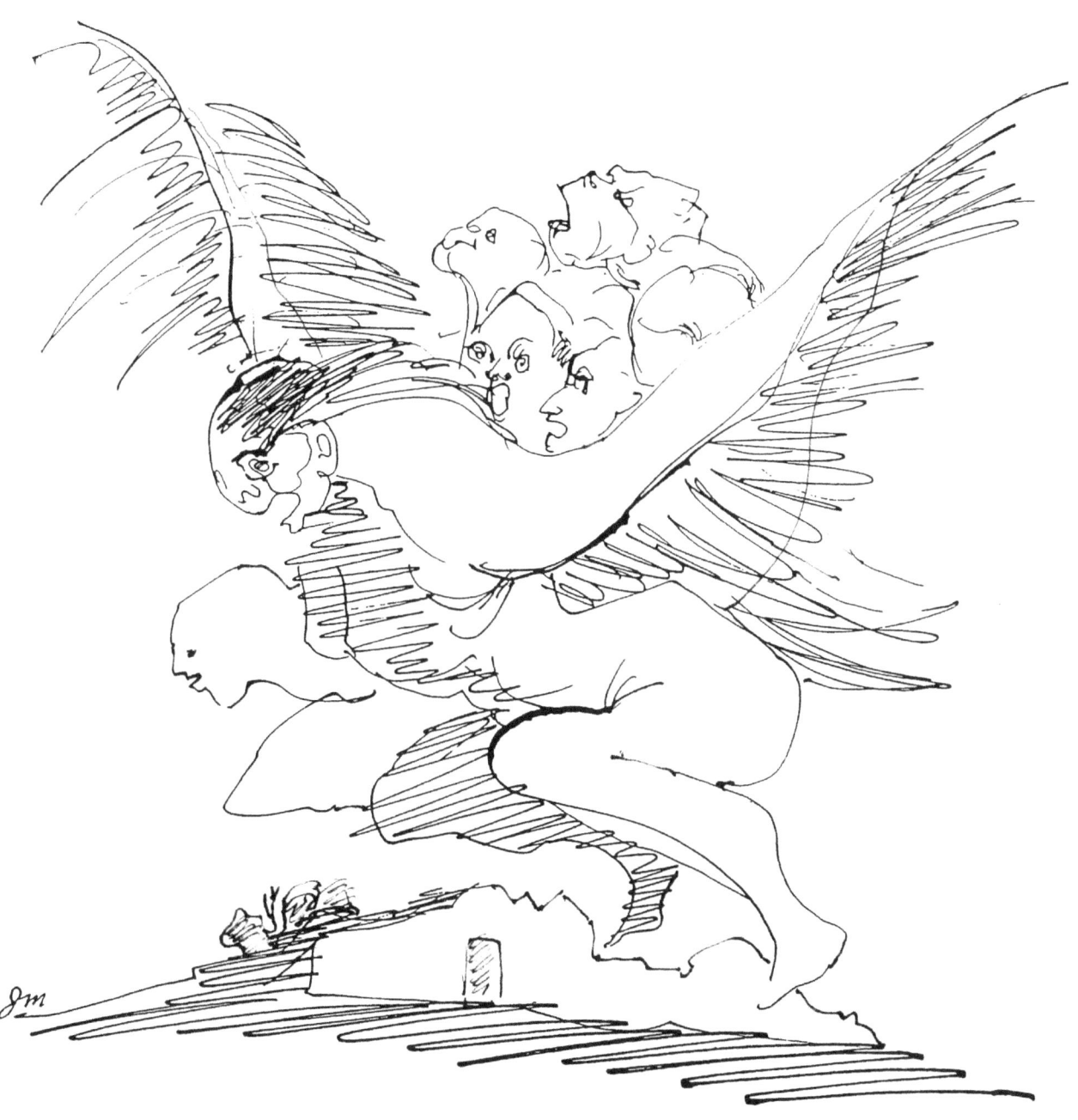

Bon Voyage!

65. Where is mama off to?

Mama has dropsy so they are taking her for an outing to entertain her.
God willing, she may recover.

¿Donde va mamá?

Mamá está ydrópica y la han mandado pasear. Dios quiera que se alibie.

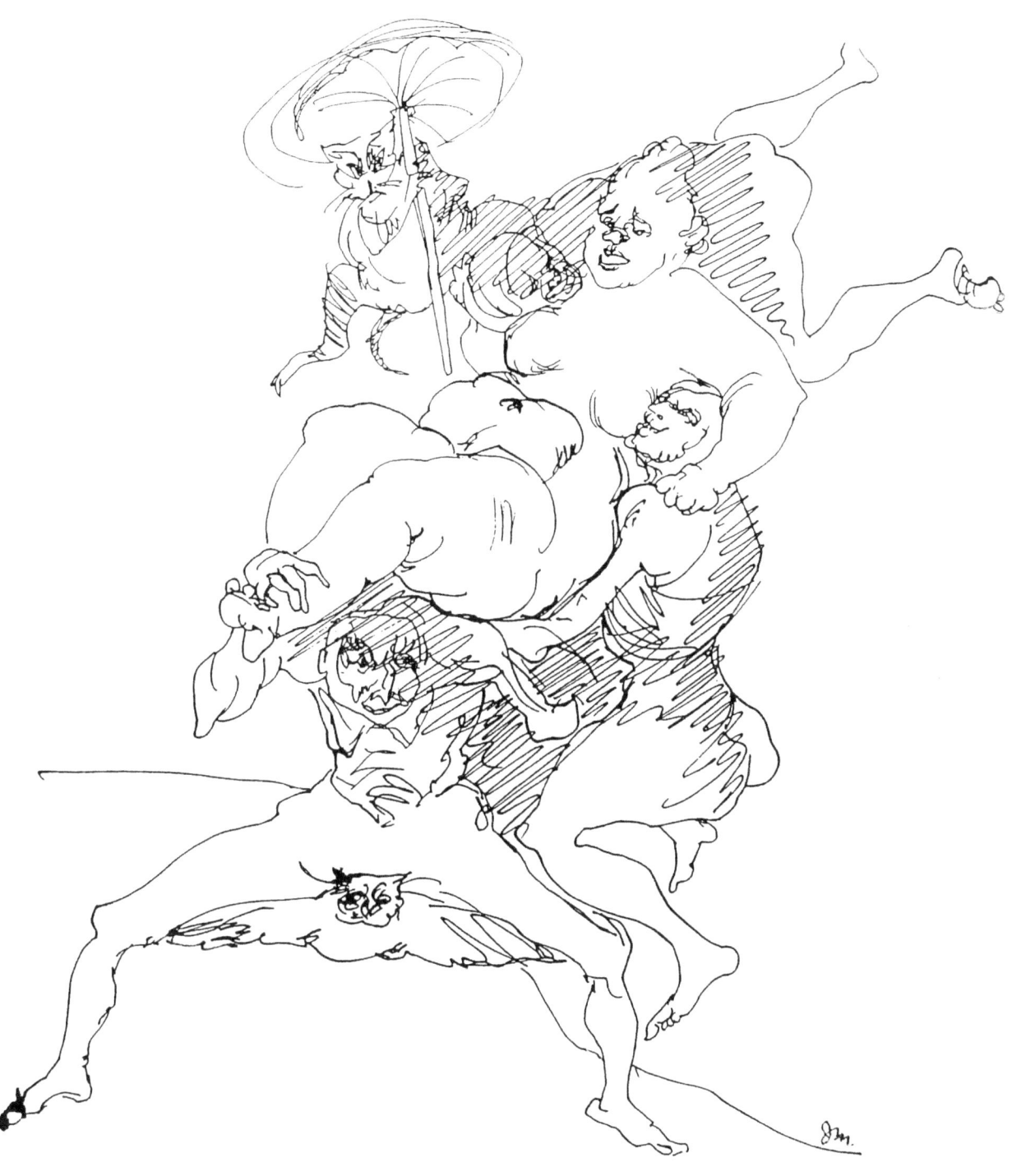

Where is mama off to?

66. Off and away!

There goes a witch with her spirit cat, riding on the crippled devil. This poor devil is the butt of jokes, but he has his uses at times.

¡Allá vá eso!

Ahi ba una bruja, a caballo en el Diablo Cojuelo. Este pobre diablo de quien todos hacen burla, no deja de ser útil algunas veces.

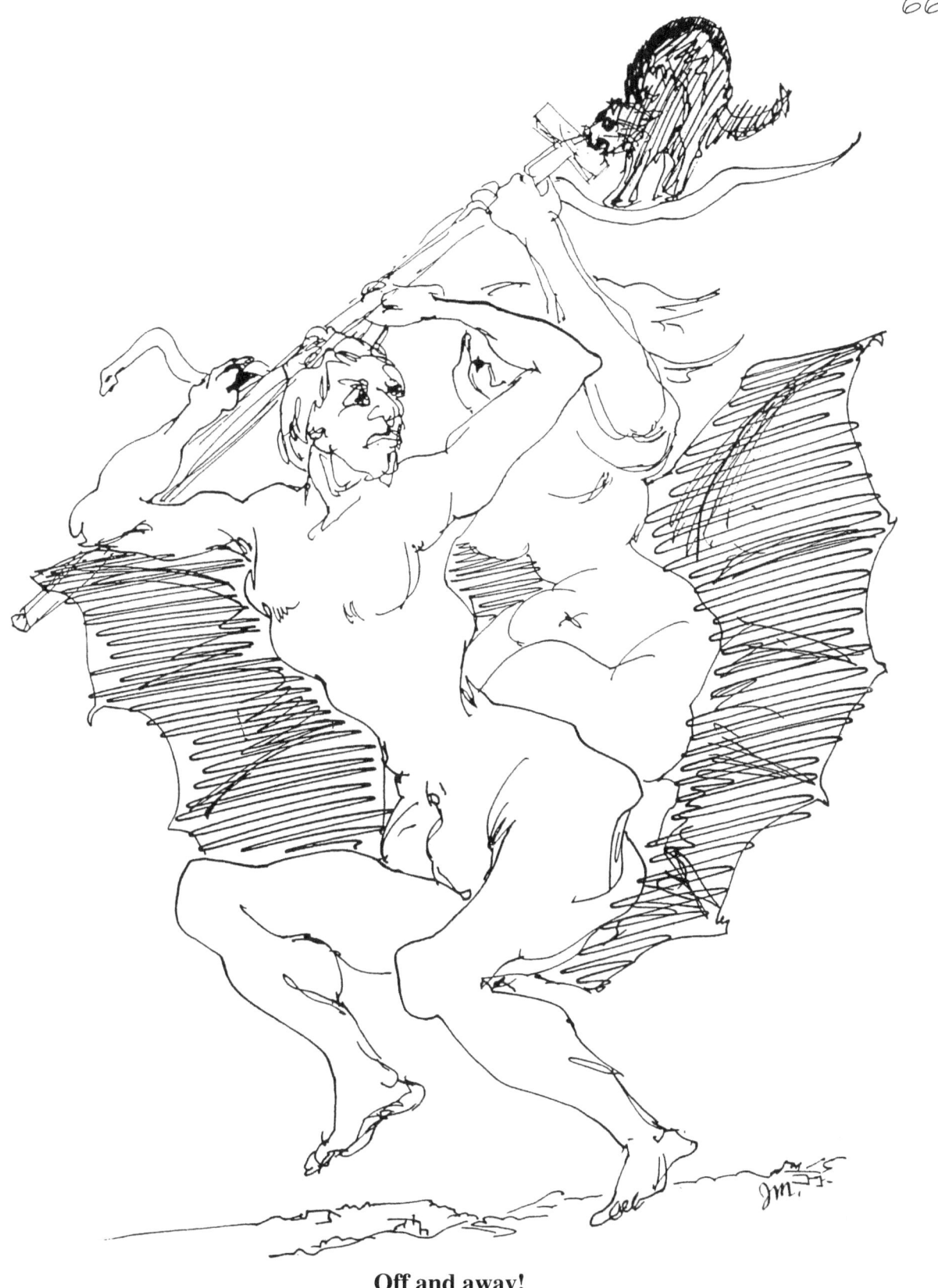

66

Off and away!

67. Wait! You're not anointed yet.

It's the same the whole world over. A silly, impatient student, even a witch, goes off half-cocked. He's being sent on an important errand but he is going to mess it up.

Aguarda que te unten.

Le embían a un recado de importancia y quiere irse a medio untar. Entre los brujos los hay también troneras, precipitados, botarates, sin pizca de Juicio: todo el mundo es país.

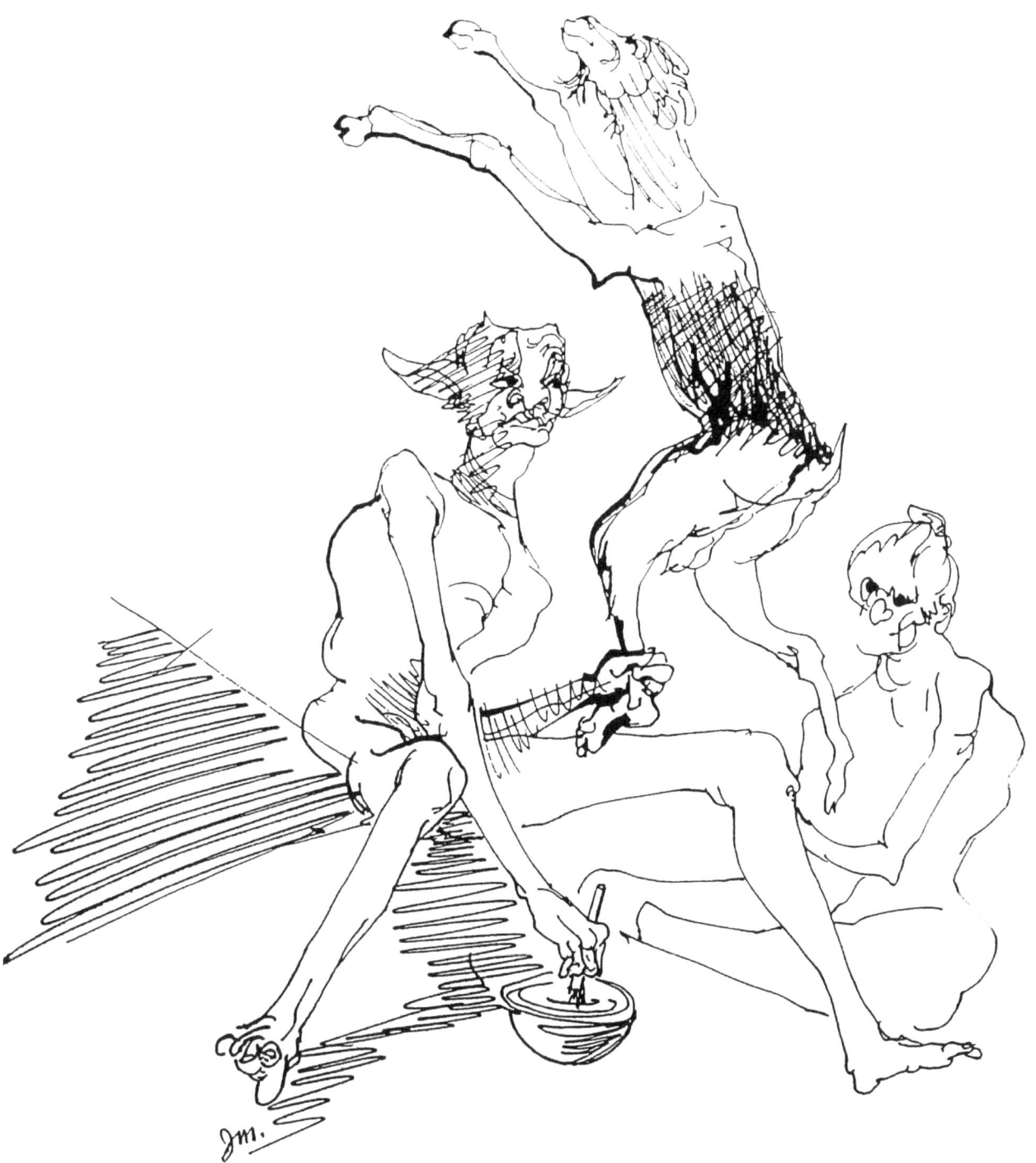

67

Wait! You're not anointed yet.

68. Nice teacher!

Witches must always have a broom, for as the legends tell, they can sometimes change
their broom into a fast mule and ride to where the Devil cannot reach them.

¡Linda maestra!

La escoba es uno de los utensilios más necesarios a las brujas porque además de ser
ellas grandes barrenderas, como consta por las istorias, talbez conbierten la escoba
en mula de pasa y van con ella que el Diablo no las alcanzara.

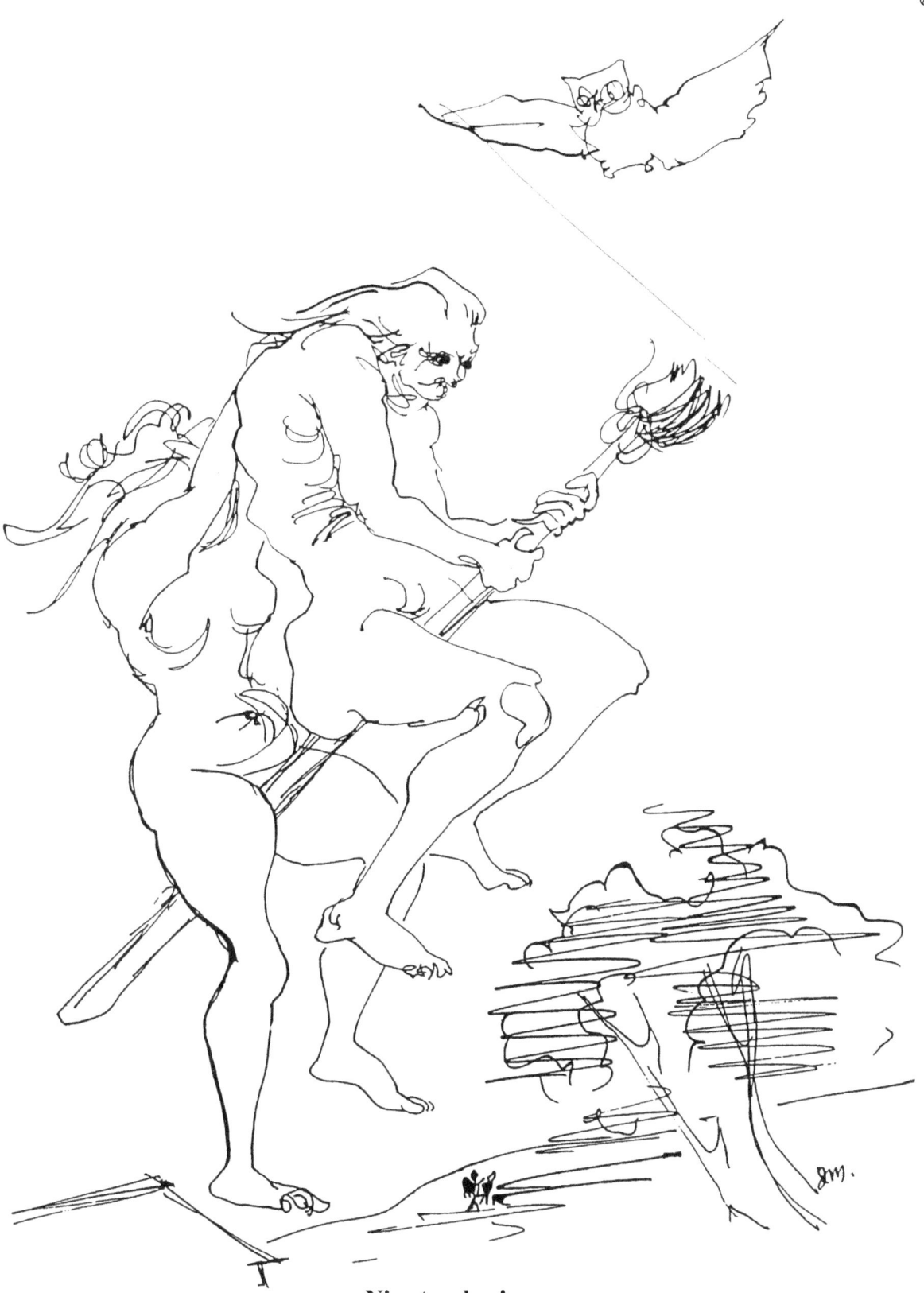

Nice teacher!

69. Blow.

The witches made a great catch of children last night. Now they are preparing a sumptuous banquet. Bon appétit!

Sopla.

Gran pesca de chiquillos hubo sin duda la noche anterior; el banquete que se prepara sera suntuso. Buen probecho.

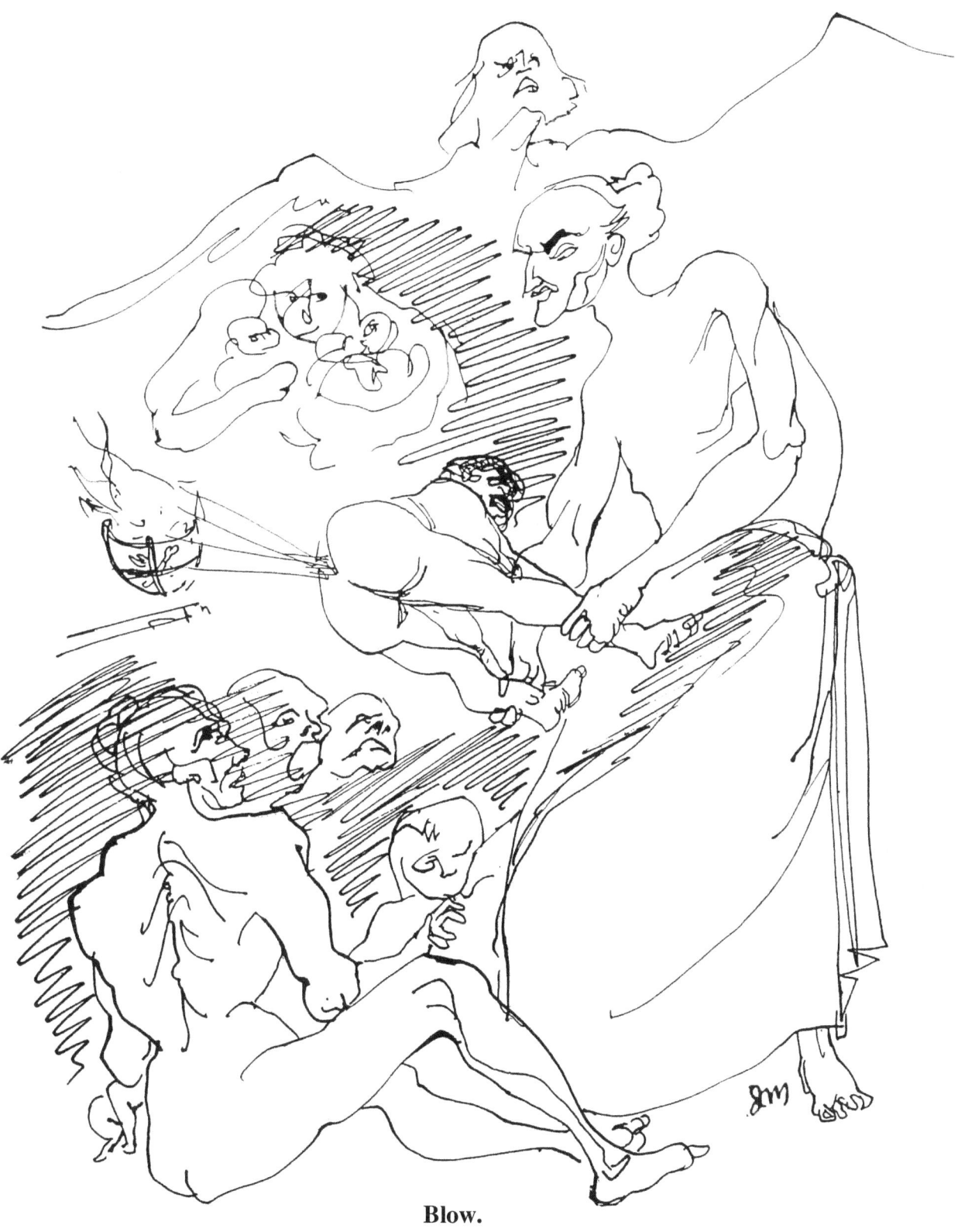

Blow.

70. Consecrated profession.

Do you swear to obey your masters and superiors? To sweep the attics, to spin rope, to ring bells, to howl, to yell, to fly, and to cook, to grease, to suck, to bake, to blow, to fry, whenever and wherever you are ordered? I swear. All right, my girl, you are now a witch. Congratulations!

Devota profesion.

¿Juras obedecer y respetar a tus maestras y superiors? Barrer desbanes, hilar estopa, tocar sonajas, ahullar, chiller, volar, quisar, untar, chupar, cocer, soplar, freir, cada y quando se te mande? Juro. Pues, hija, ya eres Bruja. Sea en ora buena.

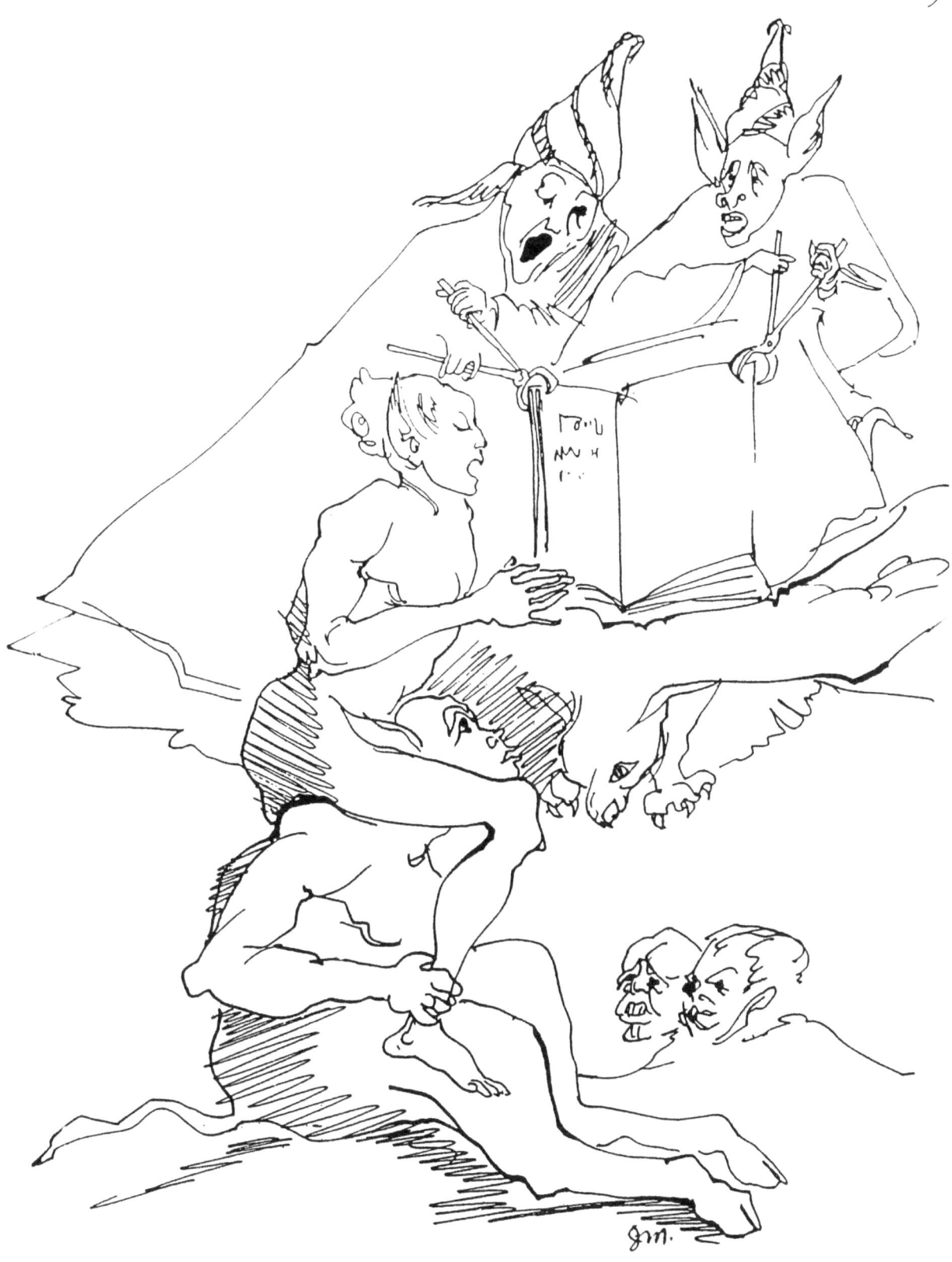

Consecrated profession.

71. Comes the dawn we'll be off and away.
If you hadn't come, nobody would have missed you.

Si amanece, nos vamos.
Y aunque no hubierais venido, no hicierais falta.

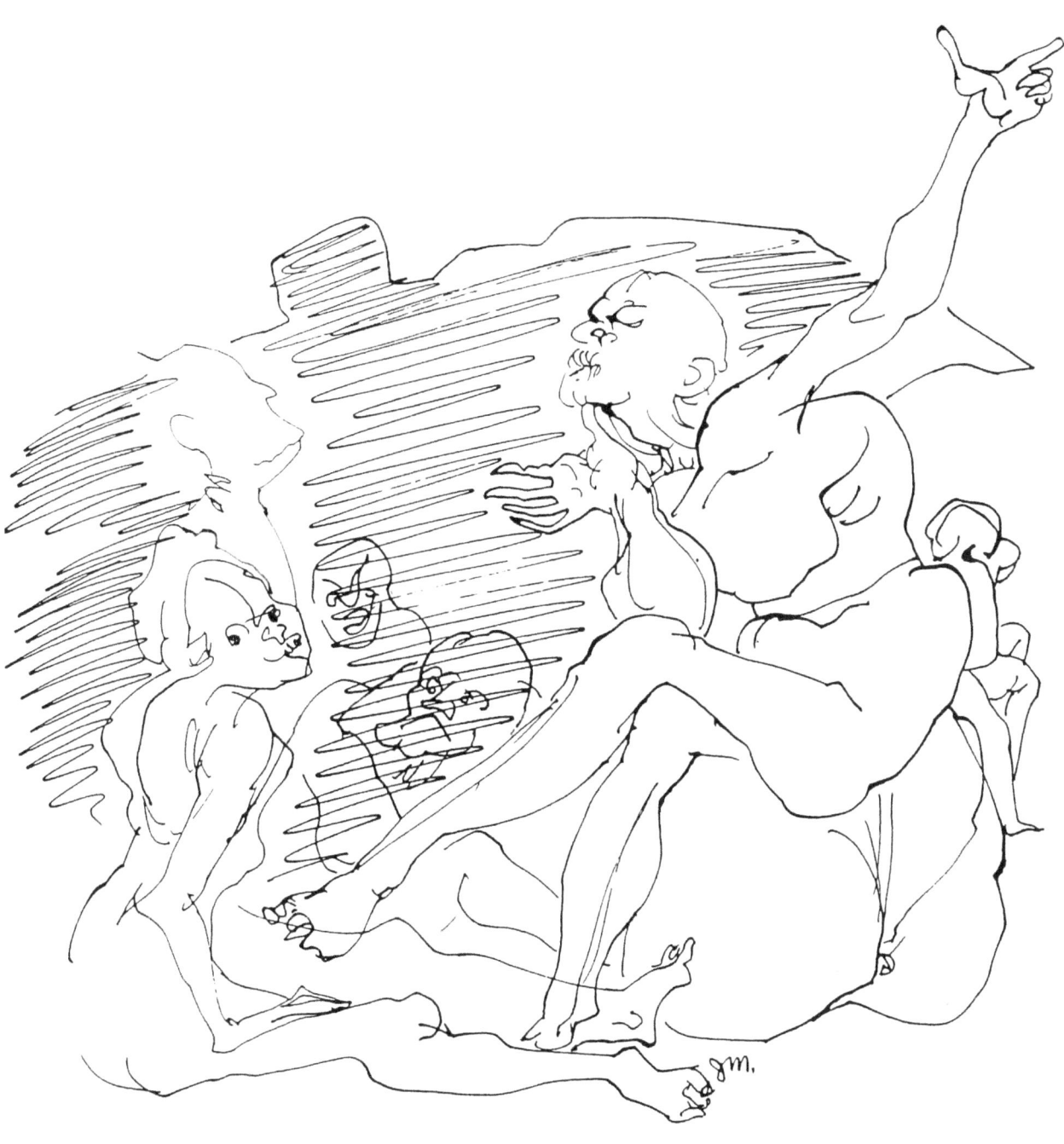

Comes the dawn we'll be off and away.

72. You won't escape.

Does she want to be caught? She plays innocent but stays in the game. She who wants to be caught will never escape.

No te escaparás.

Nunca se escapa la que se quiere dejar coger.

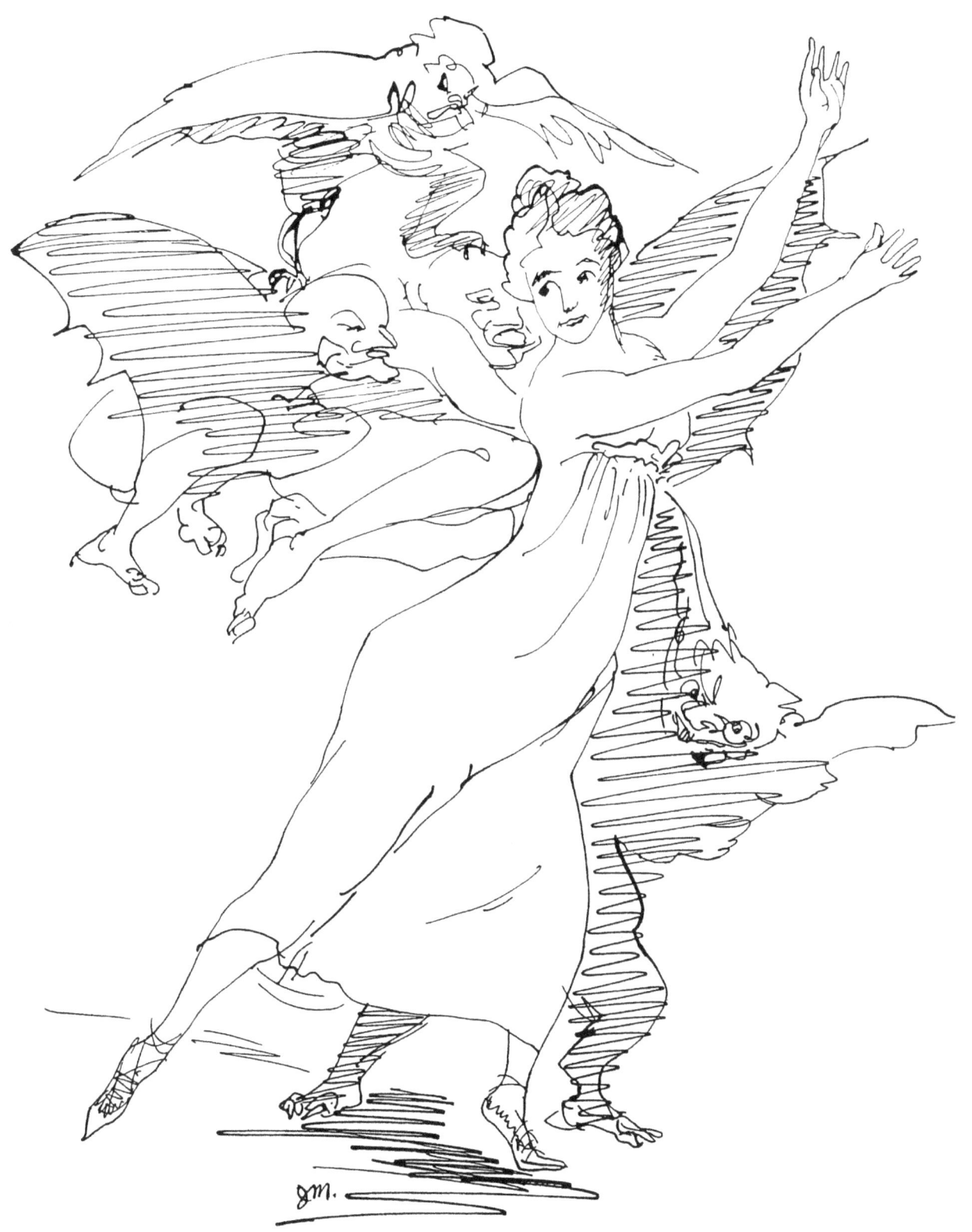

You won't escape.

73. It is better to be lazy.

If the more he works the less he gains, he is quite right to say,
"It is better to be lazy."

Mejor es holgar.

Si el que más trabaja es el que menos goza, tiene razón, major es olgar.

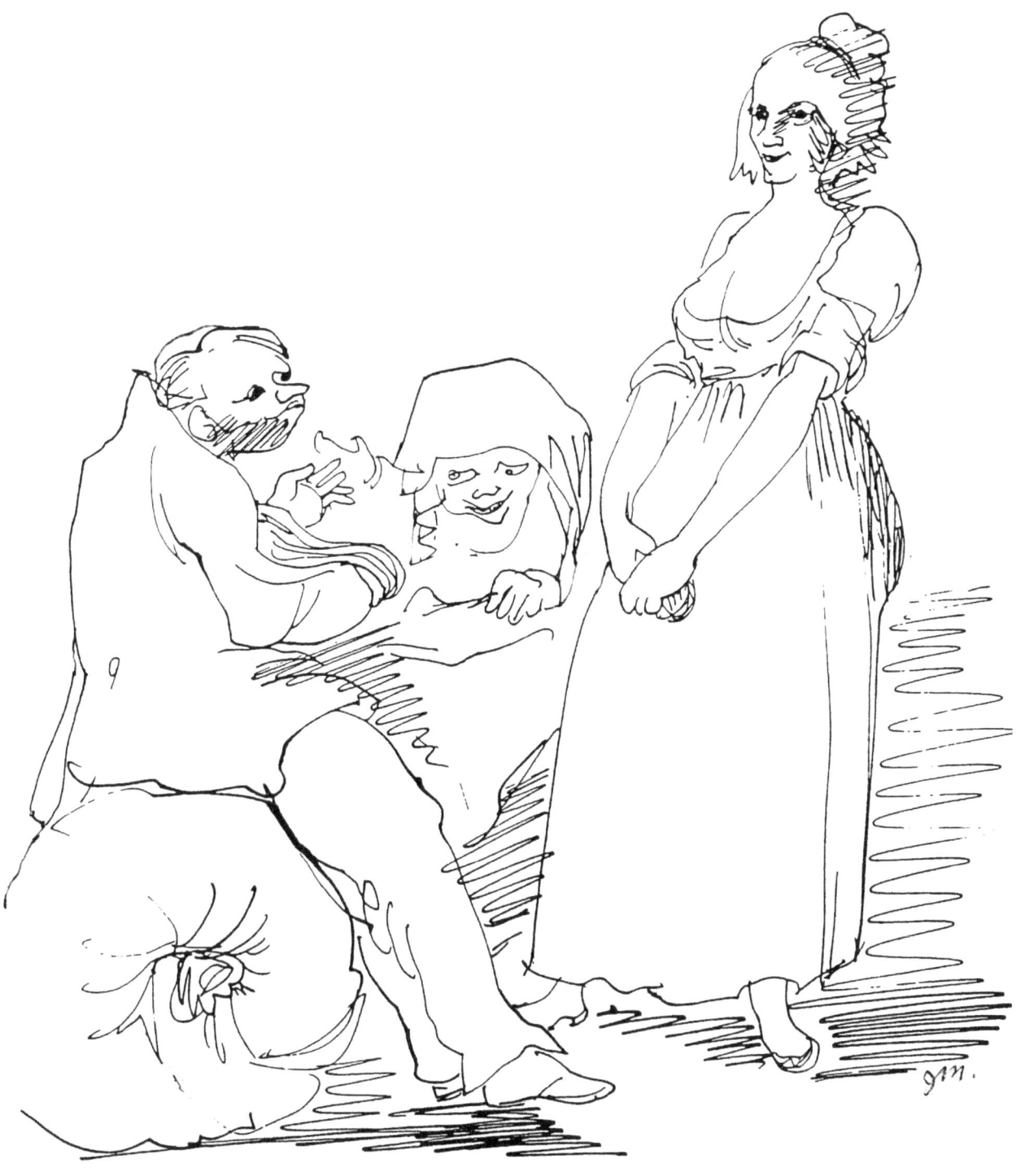

It is better to be lazy.

74. Don't scream, stupid!

Poor Paquilla! She went out looking for the footman but ran into the
goblin, Martinico, instead. But he's in a good humor and won't do her any
harm.

¡No grites, tonta!

Pobre Paquilla! Que yendo a buscar al lacayo se encuentra con el duende,
pero no hay que temer: se conoce que Martinico está de buen humor
y no le hará mal.

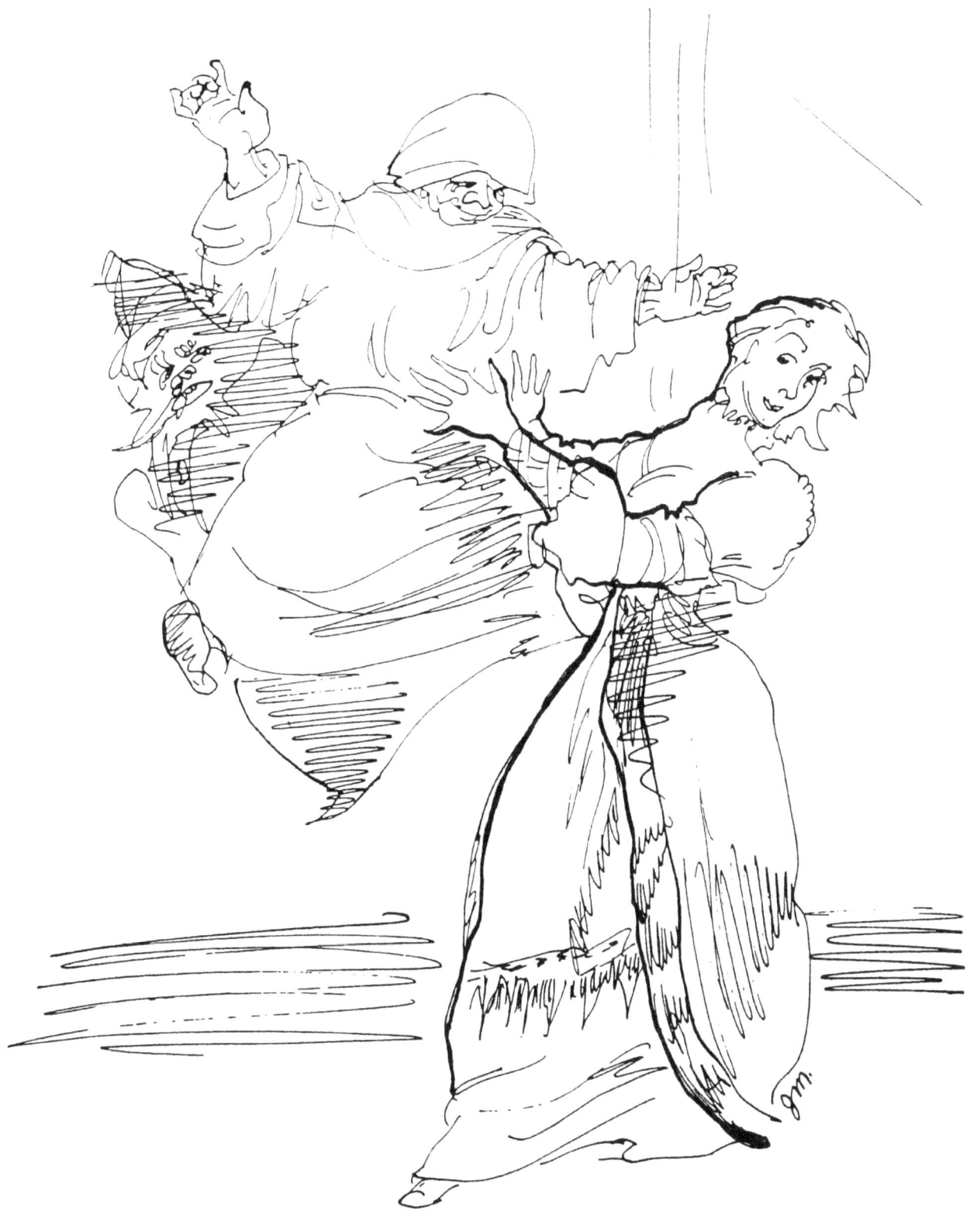

74

Don't scream, stupid!

75. Can't someone untie us?

Bound together, a man and a woman struggle to free themselves from the ropes of doctrine and cry out to be untied quickly. If I'm not mistaken these two have been forced to marry.

¿ No hay quien nos desate?

¿ Un hombre y una muger atados con sogas, forcejando por soltarse y gritando que los desaten a toda prisa? O yo me equivoco, o son dos casa - dos por fuerza.

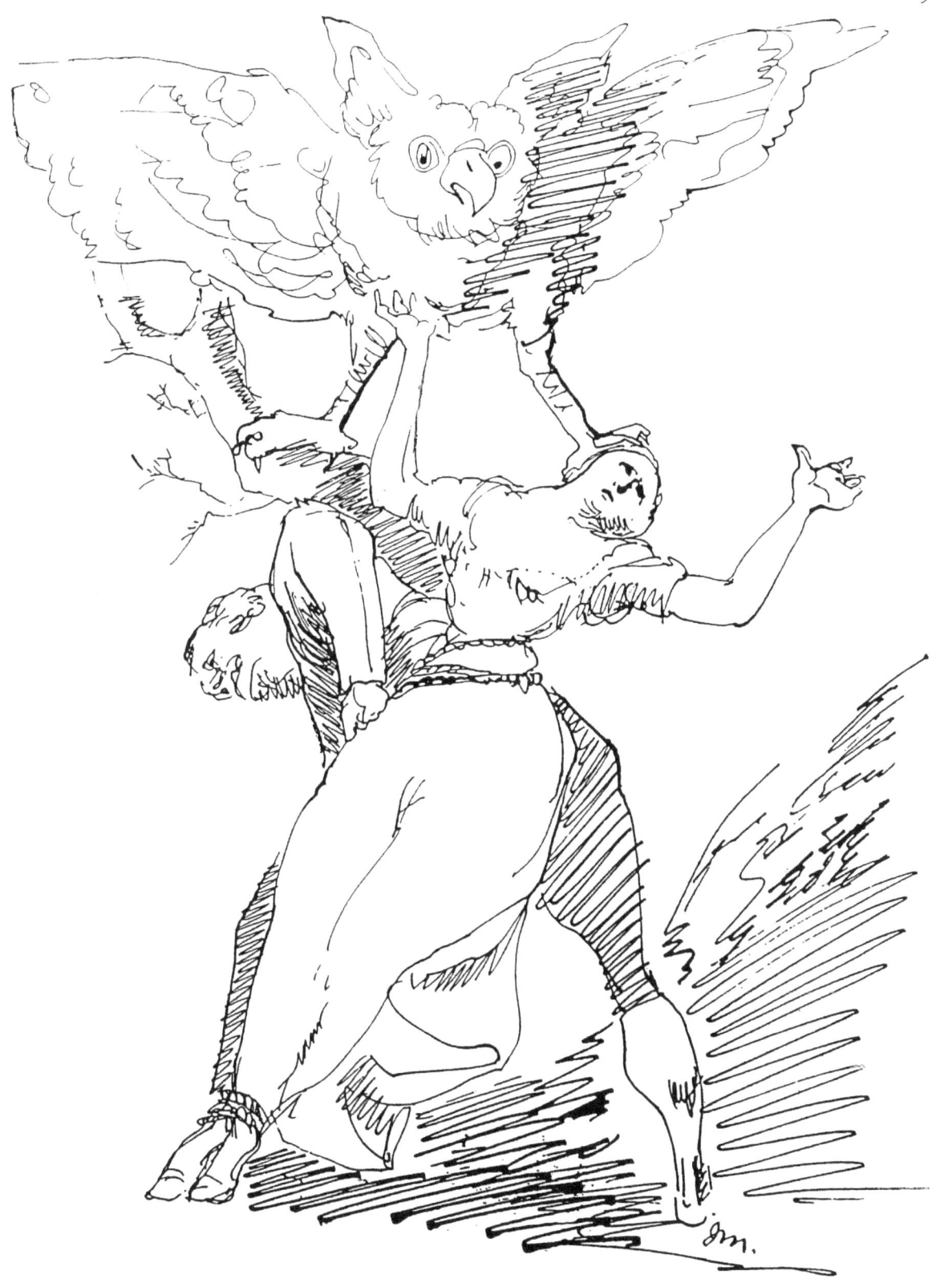

75

Can't someone untie us?

76. Watch out! Understand? Make way...look out! or else...

The cocked hat and baton convince this stupid boor that he is a superior person.
He abuses the office he was entrusted with and annoys all who know him.
He is vain and insulting with people who are his inferiors; servile and groveling with his superiors.

¿Esta um...pues, como digo...eh? ¡Cuidado! ¡Si nó!

La escarapela y el bastón le hacen creer a este majadero que es de superior naturaleza y abusa del mando que se le confía para fastidiar a quantos le conoscen; sobervio, insolente y vano con los que le son inferiores, abatido y bil con los que pueden más que él.

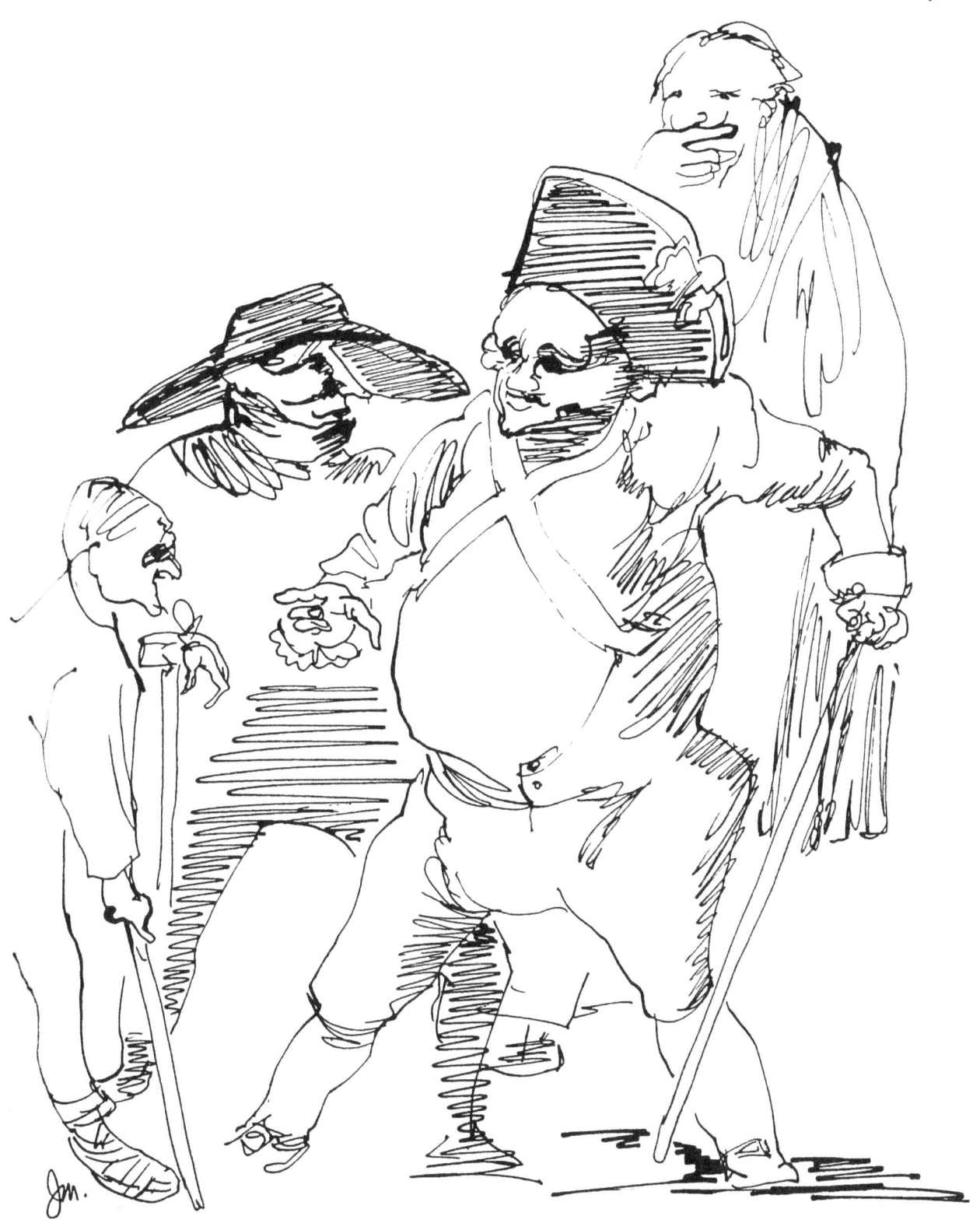

76

Watch out! Understand? Make way...look out! or else...

77. One to another.

So it goes. People insult and quarrel with one another. He who played the bull yesterday plays the bull fighter today. Fortune runs the show and assigns parts according to her changing moods.

Unos á otros.

Así va el mundo: unos á otros se burlan y se torean; el que ayer hacía de toro, hoy hace de caballero en plaza. La fortuna dirige la fiesta y distribuye los papeles según la inconstancia de sus caprichos.

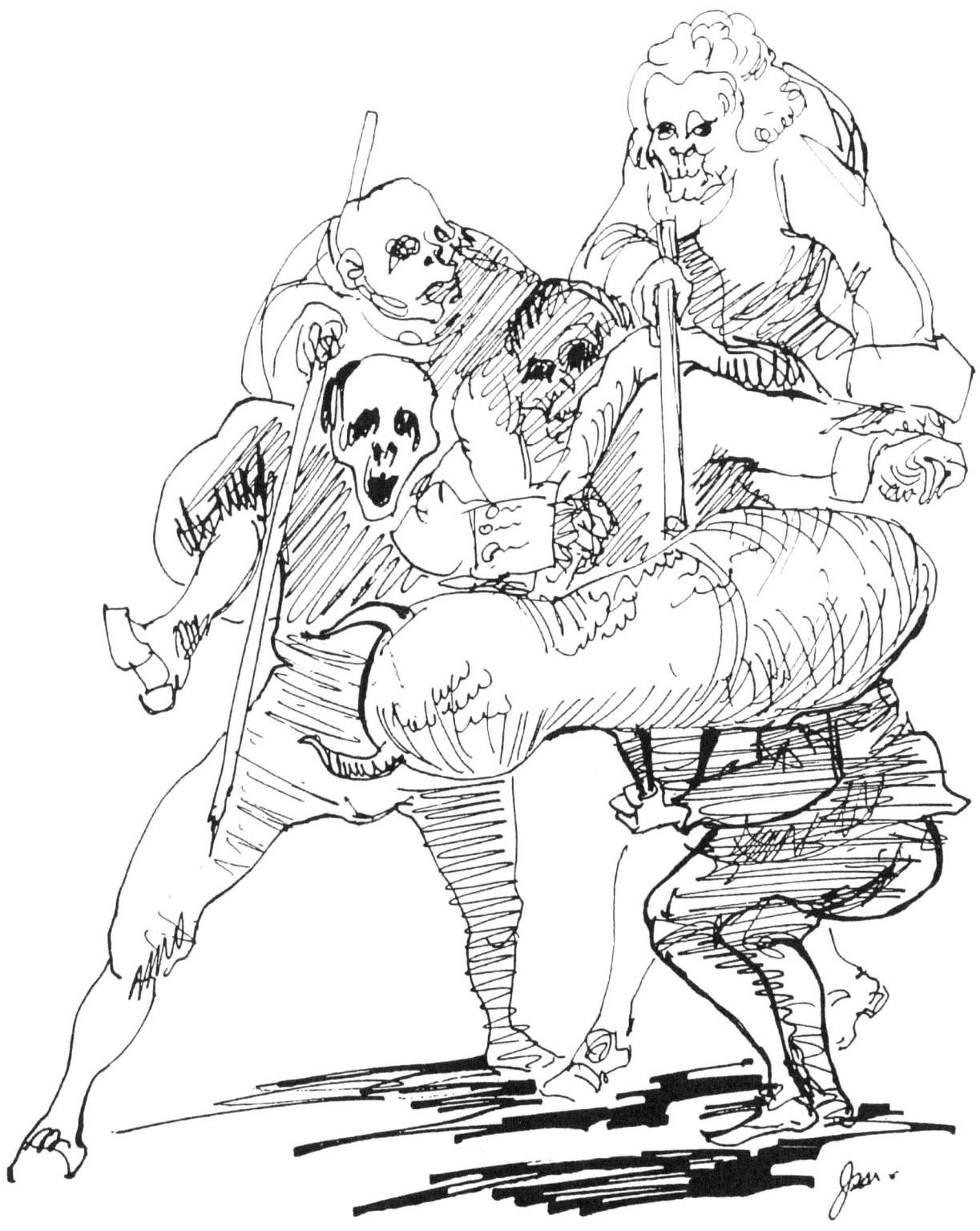

77

One to another.

78. Hurry, they're waking up.

The busiest and most helpful people are the goblins. When the maid keeps them happy they clean the pots, cook, sweep, wash up and even hush the baby. People argue over whether they are devils or not; don't be deceived. Devils are busy doing harm or preventing others from doing good, or just doing nothing at all.

Despacha, que dispiertan.

Los duendecitos son la gente más acendosa y servicial que puede hallarse; como la criada los tenga contentos, espuman la olla, cuecen la verdura, friegan, barren y acallan el niño. Mucho se a disputado si son Diablos o no; desengañemonos, los diablos son los que se ocupan en hacer mal o en estorbar que otros agan vien, o en no hacer nada.

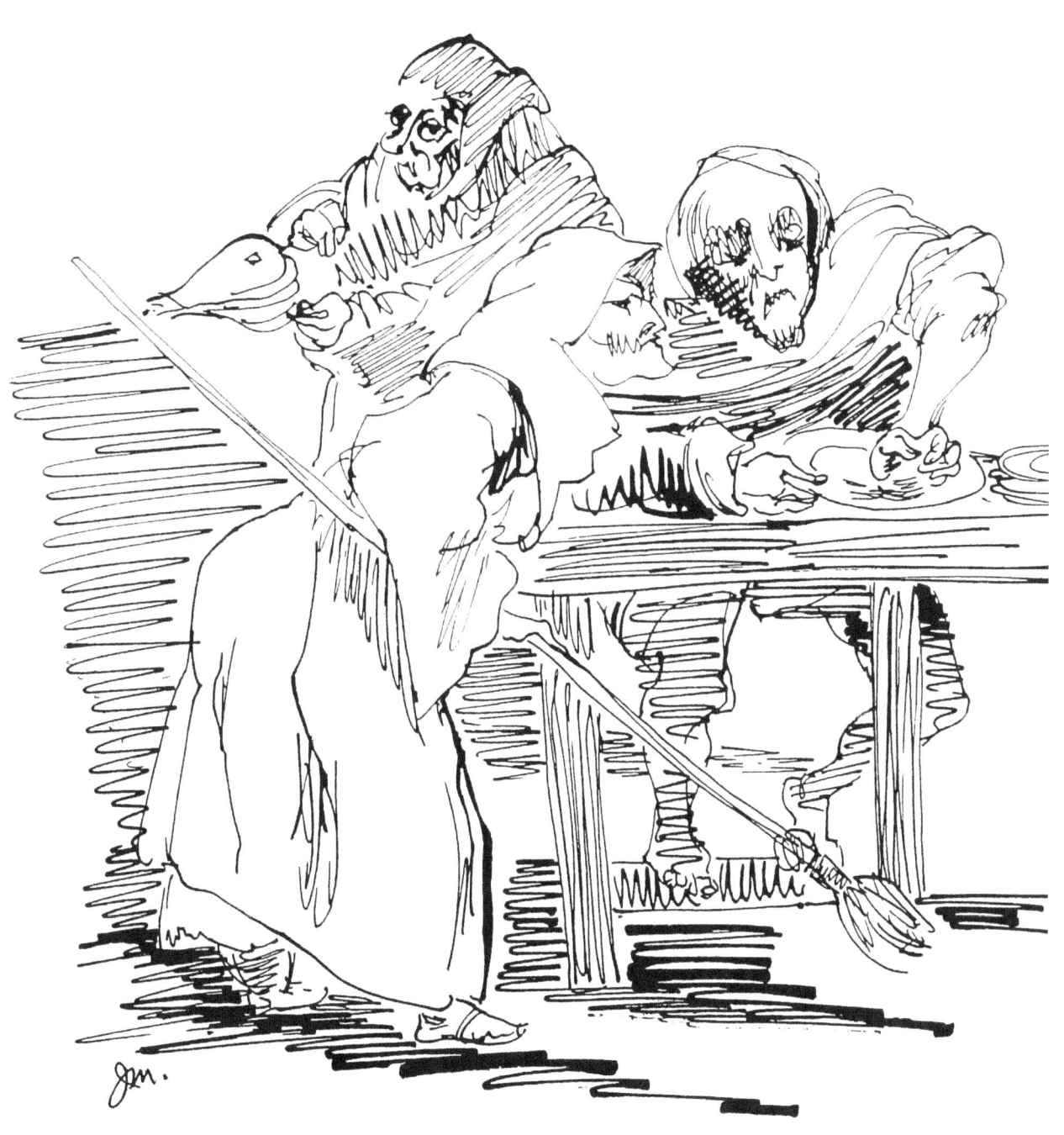

78

Hurry, they're waking up.

79. No one has seen us.

Who cares if the goblins swipe a few swigs down in the cellar if they've been cleaning up the kitchen all night and they have left it spotless and gleaming like gold?

Nadie nos ha visto.

¿Y que importa que los Martinicos baxen a la bodega y echen 4 tragos si an trabajado toda la noche y queda la espetera como una ascua de oro?

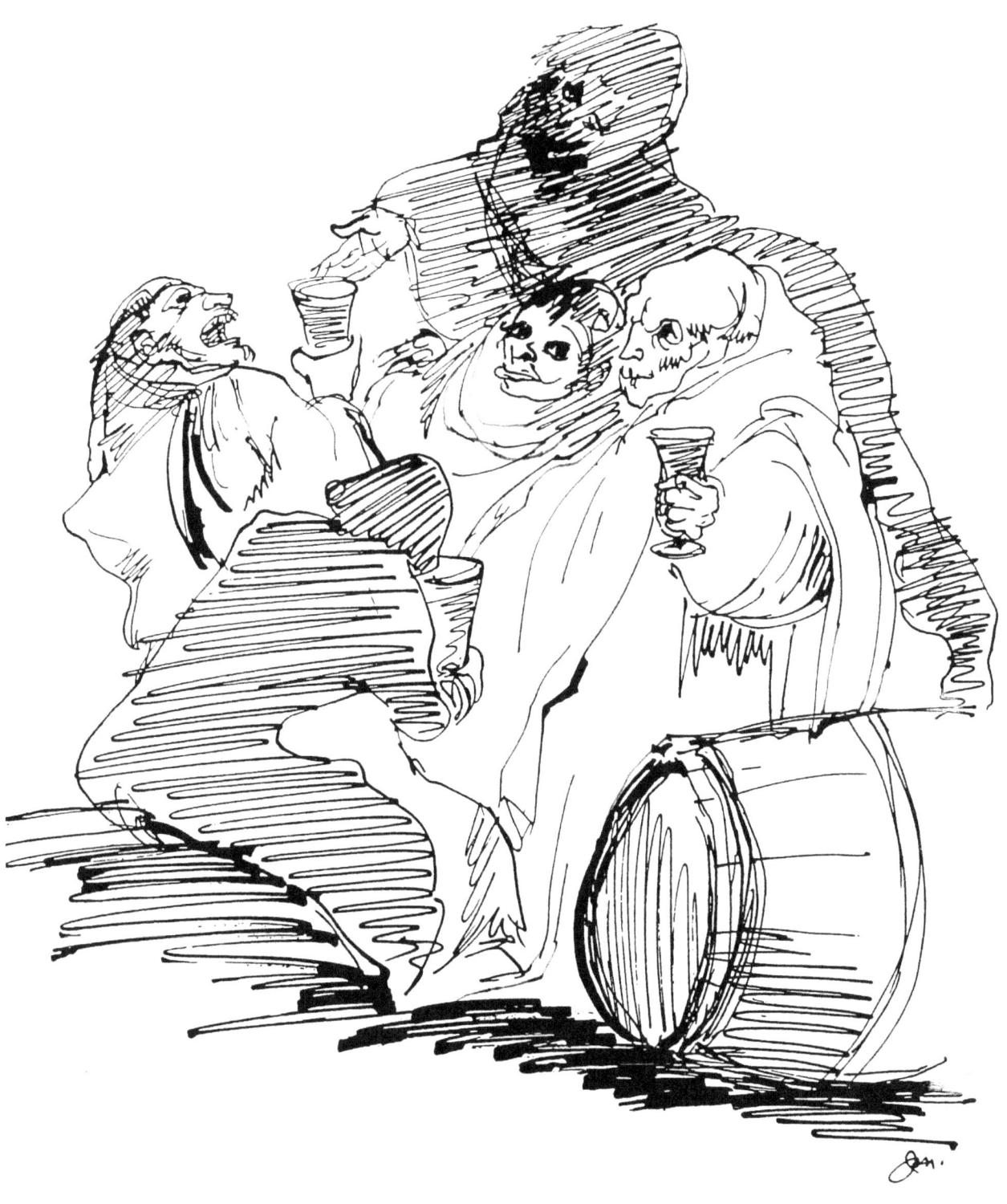

79

No one has seen us.

80. It's the hour! Time to be off.

No one has discovered where the witches, goblins and apparitions hide during the day. As soon as day breaks each one flies his own way: the witches, hobgoblins, visions and phantoms. They show themselves only in darkness. No one knows where they hide in the daytime. Anyone who could catch a group of goblins and show them in a cage at ten o'clock in the morning in the city square would not need any rights to a rich inheritance.

Ya es hora.

Luego que amanece huyen cada por su lado brujas, duendes, visiones y fantasmas. Buena cosa es que esta gente no se dexe ver sino de noche y a obscuras! Nadie a podido aberiguar en donde se encierran y ocultan durante el día. El que lograse cojer una madriguera de duendes y la enseñara dentro de una jaula a los 10 de la mañana en la Puerta del Sol, no necesitaba de otro mayorazgo.

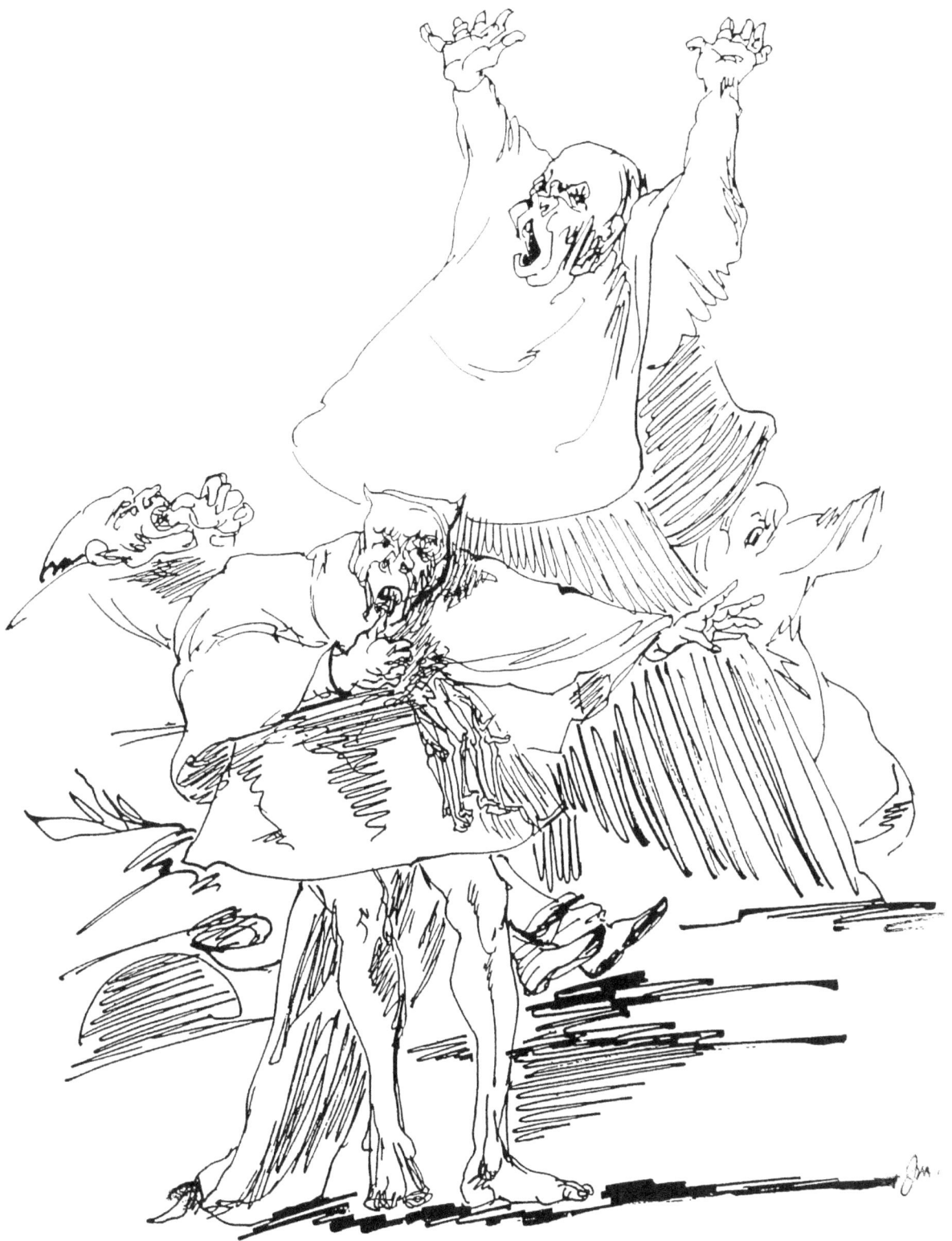

It's the hour! Time to be off.